The
JUDGES
THROUGH
KINGS
Teacher's Manual

by Emily Fischer

Designed by
Ned Bustard

www.VeritasPress.com
800-922-5082

First Edition 2001

Copyright © 2001 Veritas Press
www.VeritasPress.com
800-922-5082

ISBN 1-930710-91-7

Printed in the United States of America.

JUDGES THROUGH KINGS
How to use this Manual

We hope this guide will be helpful as you study Judges through Kings this year. You are about to take a journey through the past where you can see God's providence on a daily basis. Imagine being Deborah as she labored to lead God's people, or Samson as he wielded his great strength to defeat the Philistines. The Israelites were able to see God's glory fill the beautiful temple. God was faithful to His people through the years just as He is today. What a joy it is for young children to come to realize God's faithfulness as they learn from the past.

The *Veritas Press Bible Curriculum* was designed to be used as a tool for understanding the Scriptures and cannot be used apart from the Bible. The cards are meant to give students a smaller body of information that they can more easily assimilate. The answers to questions on the worksheets and tests can all be found on the cards, but we strongly recommend that each account is read in the Bible sometime during the week. The *Bible Reading* project is the first project for each card to encourage time spent directly in the Bible. This project reinforces the information on the card and also asks about details and facts that are not listed on the card. Teachers should encourage students to look for new information as they read from the Bible.

There are 32 events/people featured in the cards in this series. That is approximately one per week. A few of the cards have extra projects which may spread into the following week. The projects are only suggestions, so use your imagination and have fun with your group. You will note that the projects vary to appeal to different ages. You may choose the ones you think are appropriate for your group. If you are using this series for second grade or below, you may need to read some of it orally for the first six weeks; after that three times a week is usually enough. You will also want to sing the song daily for the first few weeks until it is memorized. Remember, the reason for the song is to help memorize the chronology of the events. It is also good to have the children recite events in proper order, rather than singing it after the song has been memorized. A sample school week might be planned as follows:

MONDAY: Sing the song (you may want to have a student come to the front of the room and hold up a flashcard as the class sings.) Present the new card. Read what it says on the back and discuss it. Allow different students to read it out loud if you can. Then allow the students to answer questions on the worksheet. The questions are based on information on the cards. If you are working with second grade or below, they may be asked to do this orally for the first part of the year.

TUESDAY: Sing the song. Return the graded worksheet and go over it allowing students to correct their answers. Read the account in the Bible and then complete the Bible Reading project.

WEDNESDAY: Sing the song. Orally review questions from the worksheet. Do one of the projects.

THURSDAY: Sing the song. Orally review questions from this card's worksheet and from previous events. Obviously you cannot review every question every day, so do a sampling. Assign different children different sources from the resource list on the card and allow them to look up the information and share it with the class.

FRIDAY: Give test. Use remaining time for class instruction and drill.

Having fun makes it easy to learn. Using the cards for games is one way. Ask the children to shuffle them and then see who can get their cards in order the fastest. Or have four to six students mix up their cards and then play Go Fish. This allows them to get familiar with the titles. Or you can go to a large room and see who can make their own timeline the fastest. A good way to drill questions in a classroom is to divide the children into two teams and ask questions in order. Teams receive a point for each right answer.

We have found one of the best ways to file and protect the cards is to laminate them, punch a hole in the top right corner, and keep them on a large ring. The children can add the newest card and also have the previous cards handy. Another idea is to laminate them, put Velcro strips on the card and on the wall, and start a timeline that children can put up and

JUDGES THROUGH KINGS
How to use this Manual

take down over and over again. An extra set of cards mounted at the end of the room for a reference time-line is a good idea too.

Each worksheet, test, or writing assignment should receive three grades: one each for Content, Grammar and Linguistics (Spelling).

CONTENT: On a scale of 1 to 15, a grade is given for completeness of the answer to a question. This grade is applied to their Bible grade. If your grading scale is different from 1 to 15, use yours.

GRAMMAR: The child should answer the questions in a complete sentence in which they first restate the question. For example: *What is the Scripture reference for Othniel and Ehud? The Scripture reference for Othniel and Ehud is Judges 3.* Initially in third grade the teacher may want to write a portion of the sentence on the board for the students to copy until they learn to do this correctly on their own. For example: *The Scripture reference for Othniel and Ehud is ___ .* The students would then fill in the rest. As the weeks go by gradually wean them until they are able to do this on their own. Third graders adjust to this in about six weeks. Sentences should begin with a capital letter and end with an appropriate punctua-tion mark. As the year progresses you can grade more strictly for grammar. This grade should be applied to an application grade in grammar, but should not affect Bible content grades. We suggest application at twenty percent of the overall grade.

LINGUISTICS: The children should spell all words cor-rectly. You should deduct for misspelled words once the rule for spelling a particular word has been mas-tered. For example: *I before e except after c.* Once this has been covered, a child's grade would be reduced if they spelled *priest as preist.* If they are using a Bible card to do their worksheet they should be taught that those words should be spelled correctly. This grade would be applied towards a linguistics application grade. Again we suggest twenty percent, but not to affect their Bible grade.

When you look at the tests you will see that there are not the same number of questions on each test or worksheet. We assign five points per question, with the listings of the chronology receiving two points per item listed. Partial credit may be counted because the questions are essay, and they may have portions cor-rect.

Some students may ask why they are receiving three grades on each paper. We believe that it is important for a student to realize that grammar and linguistics matter in Bible class as well as in gram-mar class. All three contribute to help make students understood by others, and are thus intertwined.

CHURCHES: We have provided pages in the back of the manual for using with this program in a Sunday school setting. These pages should be photocopied for each student and folded horizontally to cre-ate small booklets. There is more material in these booklets than can be completed during an average Sunday school time period. This calls for flexibility and creativity on the part of the Teacher. Some may even want to spread the study of a card over several weeks to cover the event in sufficient detail. Projects in the body of this manual can be used to supplement or even replace what is contained in the booklets depending on the needs of the class. Teachers should encourage parents to have their children complete the booklets, listen to the Bible song and use the flash-cards to review the information during the week to reinforce learning.

Finally we welcome your feedback and comments. We hope that this resource will enrich the education of those children entrusted to you, and will help them understand the comprehensive responsibility that God requires of them.

Judges Through Kings
Table of Contents

The Judges.................................... 7–12

Othniel and Ehud...................... 13–18

Deborah the Prophetess.............. 19–22

Gideon Delivers Israel................ 23–29

Jephthah's Foolish Vow.............. 30–35

Naomi and Ruth........................ 36–41

Samson and Delilah................... 42–51

Hannah and Eli......................... 52–58

Samuel,
The Last Judge of Israel............. 59–66

The Ark is Taken
Into Captivity........................... 67–74

Saul, The First King of Israel...... 75–82

The Genealogy of David............ 83–89

Saul's Sin at Amalek................. 90–96

David is Anointed as King........ 97–103

David and Goliath.................. 104–112

Jonathan Protects David........... 113–120

The Deaths of
Saul and Jonathan................... 121–128

Davidic Kingdom 129–135

The Conquest of
Jerusalem................................136–144

The Ark Enthroned
in Jerusalem............................ 145–151

David Writes Many Psalms....... 152–161

David and Bathsheba................ 162–171

David and Absalom 172–179

Solomon's Reign....................... 180–187

Solomon Given Wisdom........... 188–194

The Writings of Solomon......... 195–202

The Temple is Built.................. 203–211

The Queen of Sheba
Visits Solomon 212–219

The End of Solomon's Reign 220–226

Israel Divides Into
Two Kingdoms 227–234

Kings of Israel 235–241

Kings of Judah 242–249

Memory Verses......................... 251

Song Lyrics 252–255

Answers.................................. 256–275

Sunday School Handouts.......... 275–338

THE JUDGES OF ISRAEL
Worksheet

1. What is the date for the Judges of Israel?

   _____

   _____

2. List two specific sins of the Israelites in the time of the judges.

   _____

   _____

   _____

3. What does God do to punish the Israelites when they sin?

   _____

   _____

4. What does God do when the people cry out to him?

   _____

   _____

5. Who determined who would be the judge?

   _____

   _____

6. Name three major judges.

   _____

   _____

   _____

THE JUDGES OF ISRAEL
Project 1—Bible Reading

Read Judges 2. Unscramble the words below and write them in the correct blank.

dedi

hoajus

notnais

ddeerlunp

meniees

gujesd

alabs

1. Israel served the Lord until _____ died.

2. The Israelites forsook the Lord and instead served the _____.

3. God handed Israel over to their _____.

4. Israel was oppressed and _____.

5. God raised up _____ to deliver them.

6. When the judge _____ the people became corrupt again.

7. God no longer drove out the _____ which remained in the land
   when Joshua died.

THE JUDGES OF ISRAEL
Project 2—Pop-up Book

Make a book with pop-up pages as part of an ongoing project during your study of the judges. This project can be added to during the study of the following cards:

Othniel and Ehud (Card 34)
Deborah the Prophetess (Card 35)
Gideon Delivers Israel (Card 36)
Jephthah's Foolish Vow (Card 37)
Samson and Delilah (Card 39)
Samuel, the Last Judge of Israel (Card 41)

For each of these cards, the students will make a page for the book. After the last page is completed, the books will be assembled. Teachers need to check over/grade each page as it is completed. The instructor should either keep the pages for the student or instruct them as to how to safely hold onto their previous work.

How To Make Each Page:

For each page, the student needs a 8.5"x5.5" piece of paper. Fold the paper in half so that the page size is 4.25"x5.5" [1]. Cut two parallel cuts about 3/4" apart in from the folded side; only cut in 3/4" [2]. Open the page. Begin to close the page, but as you do, take your finger and push the cut portion in and crease it inside the page. Now when you open the page halfway, the cut portion pops up and looks like a chair [3]. On a separate sheet of paper, students can design and cut out a small picture. Holding the pop-up page open with the folded side horizontal, glue the small picture to the "leg" of the chair (not the "seat" of the chair).

The pop-up page will only be decorated on the two inner sides. No decoration on the outer sides will be seen when the book is assembled. Students should write their names on each page on an outer side so they do not become lost or confused.

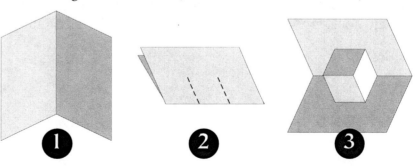

Students can make very creative and unique books if given only the minimum requirements for what is to be written or drawn on each page. On The Judges page for example, you might require students to have on their page: the date, Scripture reference, the repeated cycle, and at least three examples of judges. Students may then decide what to make pop-up, what to illustrate, and what to simply write on the page. Remind them that they could

THE JUDGES OF ISRAEL
Project 2—Pop-up Book, Page 2

have a name or Scripture reference pop-up; it does not have to always be a picture. In many cases students will choose to include more than the minimum requirements. Other possible requirements might include making it colorful, using correct spelling, and/or using complete sentences.

Let the pop-up page sit open to dry thoroughly before storing.

Once students have learned how to make the pop-up pages once, the construction of future pages goes rather quickly and requires little instruction from the teacher. After students have made one or two pop-up pages, you may show them how to make more than one thing pop-up on a page. To make two pop-ups on a page, simply make two pairs of cuts, leaving about an inch between the two sets of cuts. Then you push through the two cut portions to make two "chairs". It is not recommended that students put more than three pop-ups per page. And the pop-ups must be toward the center of the fold; they cannot be on the very top or bottom edge.

Assembly of the Pop-up Book:

When students have made all of their pop-up pages, they should put them in chronological order with all of the folds together. Teachers should page through each book to check that no page is upside down. Students will put a small amount of glue on the back of the first page. Put the glue around the outer edges and along the fold only in between the cut out portions. Important! No glue should be put on the backs of the pop-up portions as this will not allow them the freedom to pop-up as the pages are turned. Put the front of the next page to the back of the previous page. Glue all of the pages together in this fashion. To make a cover, fold a piece of construction paper in half and set the pop-up pages inside. Cut the cover a little larger than the pop-up pages and glue the cover to the pages being sure to not put any glue near the pop-up portions. Students may finally decorate the cover of their books and enjoy sharing them with their friends and family.

THE JUDGES OF ISRAEL
Project 3

Make a poster showing the cycle of events that happened over and over again in the book of Judges. Cut out the bubbles below. Fill in the blanks in the information on the bubbles. Place the first event at the top middle. Arrange the bubbles in a clockwise circle in chronological order. Glue all the bubbles in place. With crayons or markers draw arrows between the bubbles showing the clockwise direction in which the bubbles are to be read. Around the circle you may illustrate what is described in the bubbles.

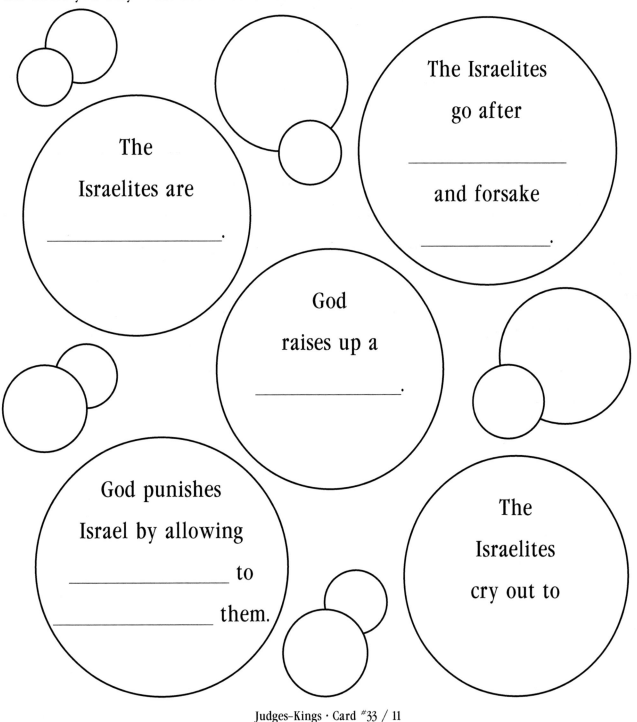

The Israelites are _____.

The Israelites go after _____ and forsake _____.

God raises up a _____.

God punishes Israel by allowing _____ to _____ them.

The Israelites cry out to

THE JUDGES OF ISRAEL
Test

1. What is the date for the Judges of Israel?

   _____

   _____

2. How were the Israelites unfaithful when they entered the Promised Land?

   _____

   _____

3. Fill in the blanks to show the pattern of Judges.

   The Israelites sin by _____

   God punishes Israel by _____

   The Israelites finally _____

   God sends a _____

   The people are _____

   But then the Israelites _____

4. Name two major judges.

   _____

   _____

OTHNIEL AND EHUD
Worksheet

1. What is the Scripture reference and date for Othniel and Ehud?

   _____

   _____

2. What king did God allow to oppress Israel because they sinned? (during Othniel's life)

   _____

   _____

3. Who was Othniel?

   _____

   _____

4. Who was Eglon?

   _____

   _____

5. Describe how Eglon was killed. (3 points)

   _____

   _____

   _____

6. What happened after Eglon was killed?

   _____

   _____

   _____

OTHNIEL AND EHUD
Project 1—Bible Reading

Read in Judges 3 about Othniel and Ehud. As you read each story you should be able to identify each part of the cycle of Judges. Write the verse in which you find each part of the cycle in the space below.

Othniel

Israel worships other gods._____

God hands Israel over to its enemies._____

Israel cries out to God._____

God sends a judge._____

Israel is freed._____

Ehud

Israel worships other gods._____

God hands Israel over to its enemies._____

Israel cries out to God._____

God sends a judge._____

Israel is freed._____

OTHNIEL AND EHUD
Project 2

Outlining is a way to organize information or take notes so that the information can quickly be read. The following are the rules for how to set up an outline.

1. Begin in line with the far left margin with Roman numeral I, II, III, etc.
2. Subcategories or points about Roman numerals I, II, III are to be labeled with capital A, B, C, etc. They are to be indented to the right under the first word behind Roman Numeral I.
3. Subcategories or points about A, B, C, etc. are labeled with 1, 2, 3, etc. and are indented to the right under the first word behind capital letter A, B, C, etc.
4. Subcategories or points about 1, 2, 3, etc. are labeled with a, b, c, etc. and are indented to the right under the first word behind 1, 2, 3, etc.

Here is a sample outline:

I. Animals
   A. Dogs
      1. Are called man's best friend
      2. Examples
         a. Terrier
         b. Poodle
         c. Collie
   B. Cats
      1. Have very good eyesight
      2. Can climb trees
II. Plants
   A. Flowers
      1. Roses
      2. Daisies
      3. Pansies
   B. Trees

Look at the outline above. Notice two more rules for outlining.

1. The first word of each line is capitalized.
2. If there is one Roman numeral there must be at least a second Roman numeral. Likewise, there must be at least two of each capital letter, number, and lowercase letter.
  * The information does not have to be in sentences.

Can you find two mistakes in the following outline?

I. Abraham
  A. His wife was Sarah.
  B. he came from the land of Ur.
  C. God made a covenant with him.
    1. He was told that his descendants would be as numerous as the sky.
    2. He was very old when God gave him his first son.
II. Isaac
  A. Married Rebecca

OTHNIEL AND EHUD
Project 2, Page 2

On this page is a complete and correct outline for this story. However, the sections of the outline are all out of order. Cut out the parts of the outline along the dotted lines. Then rearrange the pieces so that they fall under the proper heading. Once you have determined their proper order, glue them to another 8.5" x11" sheet of paper. The side edges should line up with the edge of the sheet to which they are glued. This will make your numbers and letters line up properly.

II. Ehud

A. The Moab King Eglon took over Israel because Israel sinned

B. Othniel was Israel's first judge

B. Ehud went in to see Eglon and the guards did not remove his sword because he was left-handed and carried it on his right side. Ehud said the message was secret so Eglon had his guards leave the room. Ehud took out his sword and killed Eglon. He locked the doors and escaped. Then Ehud gathered all of Israel and killed all of the Moabites so Israel was free.

I. Othniel

A. Israel did evil, so God allowed the king of Mesopotamia to enslave them. Israel repented, so God raised up a judge (Othniel) to deliver them.

Othniel and Ehud

Judges 3

Othniel and Ehud
Project 3—Covert Judge Poster

In the account written in Judges 3:12–30 we learn of the daring escapades of "Ehud, the Left-Handed Agent of God." The Bible describes how Ehud developed a secret weapon which he concealed as he went to visit the enemy. After some clever banter, he killed the villain and made a brilliant get-away.

In this light, Ehud resembles the super secret agents that have been made popular in books and movies. *Create your own movie poster advertizing a movie about Ehud's action-packed adventure, or title and color in the poster begun on the right. Include the exotic location of the story and the very fat foe.*

From BENJAMIN, *the Tribe of* BENJAMIN:

OTHNIEL AND EHUD
Test

1. What is the Scripture reference and date for Othniel and Ehud?

   _____

   _____

2. Who was the first judge?

   _____

   _____

3. Who was the king that enslaved the Israelites during Ehud's lifetime?

   _____

   _____

4. What did Ehud pretend when he went to see the king?

   _____

   _____

   _____

   _____

5. How did Ehud kill the king?

   _____

   _____

   _____

   _____

6. What did Ehud do after he killed the king?

   _____

   _____

   _____

   _____

DEBORAH THE PROPHETESS
Worksheet

1. What is the Scripture reference and date for Deborah the Prophetess?

   _____

   _____

2. In addition to being a judge, what other job did Deborah have?

   _____

   _____

3. Who was Sisera?

   _____

   _____

4. Whom did Deborah summon to lead Israel in battle? What response did she get?

   _____

   _____

5. What was the consequence of Barak's hesitance?

   _____

   _____

6. To whose tent did Sisera flee?

   _____

   _____

7. What did she do to Sisera?

   _____

   _____

   _____

DEBORAH
Project 1—Bible Reading

Read Judges 4, 5 about Deborah's time as a judge. Then put the adjectives or descriptive phrases below under the name of the person that they describe.

Received a drink from his killer | sat under a palm tree | killed Sisera |
had 900 chariots of iron | commander of the enemy army |
commander of the Israelite army | prophetess | called the enemy to her tent |
would not go by himself | judge | King of Canaan | ran away on foot |

Deborah

_____

_____

Barak

_____

_____

Jabin

_____

_____

Jael

_____

_____

Sisera

_____

_____

DEBORAH THE PROPHETESS
Project 2

When Israel routed Jabin's army, his commander, Sisera, fled on foot to Jael's tent. Label and illustrate this picture of Jael's tent. First cut out the tent below. Cut along the dashed lines so that the tent door can be lifted up. Glue the tent to another sheet of paper, but do not glue down the door.

Write labels for the following parts of a tent used during Jael's time:

TENT DOOR: a flap of cloth that could be raised and lowered.
   The only man allowed inside a tent was the father of the family.

TENT POLES: wooden poles that were stuck in the ground

COVERINGS: cloth or goats' hair that was stretched over the tent poles and tied down with cords. The coverings would shrink after rain fell on it so that it was then waterproof.

TENT PEGS: wooden pegs which pulled tight the cords and coverings. The pegs were hammered into the ground.

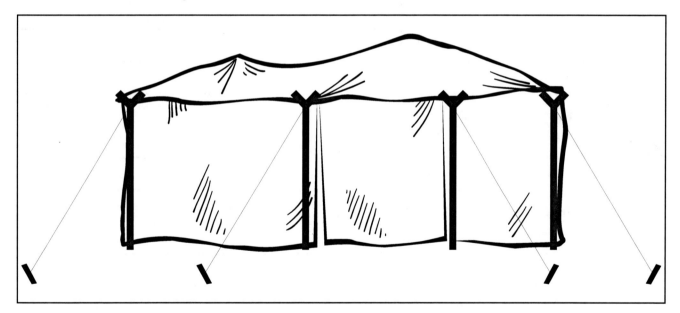

Now draw under the tent door flap the following things that could be found inside a tent:

FIRE HOLE: a hole dug in the ground in the middle of the tent. The fire hole was where the family cooked their food.

COOKING POTS AND GOATSKIN BOTTLES: Food was kept inside the tent in pots, and water and milk were kept in bottles made from goatskins.

STRAW MATS AND ANIMAL SKINS: Mats made from straw were used as places to sit and animal skins were used for tables.

DEBORAH THE PROPHETESS
Test

1. What is the Scripture reference and date for Deborah the Prophetess?

    _____

    _____

2. In addition to being a judge, what other job did Deborah have?

    _____

    _____

    _____

3. Who was Barak?

    _____

    _____

4. Why wouldn't Barak receive the glory of capturing the leader of the Canaanite army?

    _____

    _____

    _____

5. Who was the leader of the Canaanite army?

    _____

    _____

6. Why did the enemy leader go into Jael's tent?

    _____

    _____

7. How did Jael kill the enemy leader?

    _____

    _____

    _____

GIDEON DELIVERS ISRAEL
Worksheet

1. What is the Scripture reference and date for Gideon Delivers Israel?

   _____

   _____

2. What sign did Gideon ask of God before he went into battle with the Midianites?

   _____

   _____

   _____

3. What two groups of people did Gideon send away from the army?

   _____

   _____

   _____

GIDEON DELIVERS ISRAEL
Worksheet, Page 2

4. Why did God have Gideon reduce the number of men that would go into battle?

   _____

   _____

   _____

5. With how many men did Gideon go into battle?

   _____

   _____

   _____

6. At what time of day did Gideon and his men attack the Midianites?

   _____

   _____

   _____

7. How did the Israelites defeat the Midianites?

   _____

   _____

   _____

   _____

GIDEON DELIVERS ISRAEL
Project 1—Bible Reading

Read about Gideon in Judges 6:11-7:21. Then fill in the spaces in the outline below.

I. Gideon leads spiritually.

v.25   A. Gideon's _____ built an altar to _____ and an Asherah that the

    people _____.

      1.   God told Gideon to _____

v.27   2.   Gideon goes _____ because he is afraid of _____.

v.28 B. The people find the altar and the Asherah _____.

      1.   They found out that Gideon destroyed them and wanted to _____.

v.32 2.   Gideon's _____ said to let Baal _____.

II. Gideon leads militarily

  A. Gideon asks for a _____.

      1.   Gideon says if the fleece is _____ and the ground is _____

         in the morning he will know that God _____.

      2.   In the morning the _____ is _____ and the _____ is

         _____. Gideon then asks that the next morning the

         _____ be _____ and the _____ be

         _____. God _____ this sign.

  B. Gideon chooses his men.

      1.   God wants all of the glory.

      2.   God tells Gideon that he has too many _____.

         a. Gideon sends away all that are _____.

         b. Gideon sends away all that _____.

      3.   Gideon goes into battle with _____ men.

  C. Gideon defeats the _____

      1.   The men went to the camp of the Midianites blowing _____,

         smashing _____, and carrying _____.

      2.   The Midianites thought there were more Israelites than there actually

         were, so they _____.

      3.   The Israelites chased down the Midianites and _____.

GIDEON DELIVERS ISRAEL
Project 2

Make a poster showing how God used the fleece to confirm his word to Gideon.

Give each student a 4"x11" piece of fleece, felt, or soft material and a photocopy of "Gideon" written backwards (see next page). Have students glue the Gideon letters to the wrong side of the fleece. Students will cut out the backward letters and fleece. Students may need sharper scissors depending on the weight of the material that you select. On another sheet of paper, students will glue the letters with the fleece side up to spell Gideon. The background may be decorated to look like ground. Have students draw a line to divide their paper and the word Gideon in half (between the d and the e). Use blue construction paper to cut out many water droplets. On the left half of the paper glue water droplets to the fleece but not the ground. On the right half glue water droplets to the ground but not the fleece.

To make an even fancier poster, give students another piece of paper that is larger than the piece to which they glued the letters. Center the letters page so that the new piece of paper provides a border of at least an inch. In the border, students may draw pictures, symbols, or decorations depicting other parts of Gideon's story.

GIDEON DELIVERS ISRAEL
Test

1. What is the Scripture reference and date for Gideon Delivers Israel?

   _____

   _____

2. Gideon put a _____ on the ground at _____.

   In the _____ the ground was _____ and the

   _____ was _____.

3. What two groups of people did Gideon send away from the army?

   _____

   _____

4. Why did God have Gideon reduce the number of men that would go into battle?

   _____

   _____

5. With how many men did Gideon go into battle?

   _____

   _____

6. At what time of day did Gideon and his men attack the Midianites?

   _____

   _____

7. How did the Israelites defeat the Midianites?

   _____

   _____

   _____

   _____

GIDEON DELIVERS ISRAEL
Test, Page 2

Review

1. Name three major judges.

_____

_____

_____

_____

2. Who was Othniel?

_____

_____

_____

_____

3. Who was Sisera?

_____

_____

_____

_____

4. To whose tent did Sisera flee?

_____

_____

_____

JEPHTHAH'S FOOLISH VOW
Worksheet

1. What is the Scripture reference and date for Jephthah's Foolish Vow?

   _____

   _____

2. From what nation did God deliver the Gileadites by raising up Jephthah?

   _____

   _____

3. Why were the Ephraimites angry with the Gileadites?

   _____

   _____

   _____

4. Who won the battle between the Gileadites and the Ephraimites?

   _____

   _____

5. How did Jephthah and the Gileadites determine who the Ephraimite survivors were?

   _____

   _____

   _____

Jephthah's Foolish Vow
Worksheet, Page 2

6. What had Jephthah vowed to God?

   _____

   _____

7. What happened when Jephthah returned from battle victorious?

   _____

   _____

   _____

   _____

8. What happened to Jephthah's line because of his vow?

   _____

   _____

   _____

   _____

Jephthah's Foolish Vow
Project 1—Bible Reading

Read about Jephthah in Judges 11:1-12:7. Then fill in the spaces in the outline below.

I. Jephthah's background

   A. He was a Gileadite. His father was _____.

   B. His mother was a _____.

   C. His brothers chased him _____.

II. Jephthah delivers Israel

   A. Jephthah sends _____ to the king of the _____

      asking him to give back the _____ he had taken from _____.

      The _____ king would not listen to Jephthah.

   B. Jephthah _____ to God that if God gave him the victory, he would

      _____ whatever first came _____.

   C. God gives Israel _____.

   D. Jephthah's _____ comes out to meet him when he returns victorious.

     1. She told him to do to her as he had vowed to God.

     2. She requested to have _____ to _____ with her

        _____ because she would never _____.

III. _____ turn against Jephthah

   A. They complain that Jephthah never gave them a chance

      to join in the _____.

    (They had similarly complained to _____ in Judges 8:1.)

   B. Ephraim attacked Jephthah and his men.

     1. Jephthah _____ them.

     2. When _____ tried to cross the _____ to return to

       _____, the Gileadites made them say the word _____.

      a. Ephraimites could not _____ the word _____

       correctly.

      b. The men of Gilead _____ all that said _____

       instead of _____.

Jephthah's Foolish Vow
Project 2—Timbrel

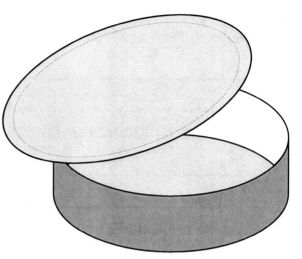

Jephthah vowed that if God would grant Israel military success, he would sacrifice the first living thing that he saw come out of his house. When he returned home victorious, his daughter came out to greet him playing the timbrel. The timbrel is a musical instrument made of a wooden hoop with animal hides stretched over the top and bottom. It is played by hitting the stretched hides with one hand while holding it in the other hand. *Have students make a small model of a timbrel. You will need a round oatmeal box, sheet of cardboard, paint, and hot glue. Cut the top off the oatmeal box leaving about a two inch band attached to the top. Lay the top on the cardboard sheet and trace around the edge. Cut the cardboard sheet about 1/2 inch larger than the tracing. Hot glue the cardboard circle to the band of the oatmeal box. Allow the glue to dry before painting or decorating your timbrel.*

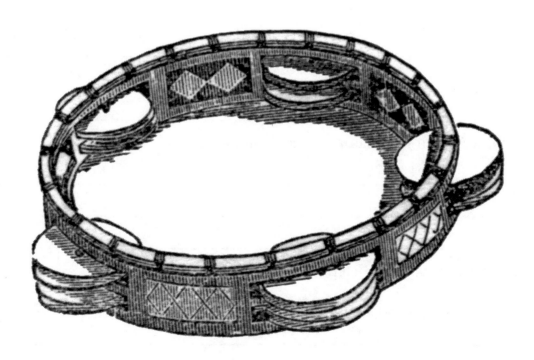

JEPHTHAH'S FOOLISH VOW
Test

1. What is the Scripture reference and date for the story of Jephthah?

   _____

   _____

2. Whom did Jephthah lead against the Ammonites?

   _____

   _____

3. About what did the Ephraimites complain to Jephthah? Why did they have no right
   to complain?

   _____

   _____

   _____

4. How did Jephthah determine who the Ephraimite survivors were?

   _____

   _____

5. What did Jephthah vow to God?

   _____

   _____

   _____

6. What happened when Jephthah returned from battle?

   _____

   _____

   _____

7. What may have happened to Jephthah's daughter?

   _____

   _____

Jephthah's Foolish Vow

Test, Page 2

Review

1. Why did God send the judges?

   _____

   _____

2. Who was Eglon?

   _____

   _____

3. What did Jael do to Sisera?

   _____

   _____

   _____

   _____

4. Who was Barak?

   _____

   _____

5. With how many men did Gideon fight against the Midianites?

   _____

   _____

NAOMI AND RUTH
Worksheet

1. What is the Scripture reference and date for Naomi and Ruth?

   _____

   _____

2. How was Ruth related to Naomi?

   _____

   _____

   _____

3. Where did Naomi and Ruth go after the men in the family died?

   _____

   _____

   _____

4. What does the name Mara mean?

   _____

   _____

5. Who left grain for Ruth so that she and Naomi could survive?

   _____

   _____

6. What did Ruth do to make Boaz decide that he wanted to marry her?

   _____

   _____

   _____

   _____

Naomi and Ruth
Worksheet, Page 2

7. Whom did Boaz have to talk to before he
   could possibly marry Ruth?

   _____

   _____

   _____

   _____

8. How were Ruth and Boaz related to King
   David? Who is the most famous person
   that descended from Ruth?

   _____

   _____

   _____

   _____

   _____

9. What does a kinsman-redeemer do?

   _____

   _____

   _____

   _____

NAOMI AND RUTH
Project 1—Bible Reading

Read about Naomi and Ruth in Ruth 1-4. Then fill in the spaces in the outline below.

I. The characters

    A. Naomi: an Israelite woman who went to _____ with her two _____.
       Her sons married _____ women, and then both sons and Naomi's
       _____died.

    B. Ruth: a _____ woman who married one of _____ sons.
       She left her parents and home to stay with _____.

    C. Boaz: a close _____ of Naomi

II. The problem

    A. Naomi lost both sons and her husband. She was in a _____ country.

    B. There was a famine so Naomi returned to _____ where she hoped she
       could find _____. In Israel you were only allowed to pick your field
       once. Anything that was missed was to be available to the poor and widows.
       Naomi sent _____ to search for grain after the pickers.

III. The solution

    A. Boaz saw _____ in his fields and commanded his workers to help her.

      1. He let her _____ and _____ with his workers.

      2. He had his workers purposely leave behind _____ for her to get.

    B. _____ tells Ruth to lie down at _____.

    C. Boaz will redeem Ruth.

      1. When a husband died and their was no son to carry on the line, the closest
          relative would marry the widow to produce a son to carry on the line.

      2. There was another closer _____ than Boaz who had the first
        option of _____ Ruth.

      3. Boaz went to the other _____ and in front of
        _____ he gave that man the choice of buying the
        _____ from _____ and marrying _____.

      4. The closer relative did not want to do this, so Boaz did. Boaz removed his
        _____ and _____ it to the other man to show that
        the matter was _____.

      5. _____ married Ruth and they had a _____.

    D. The son of _____ and _____ was named _____.
       He was the _____ of David.

Naomi and Ruth
Project 2—Grain Farming

Boaz was a farmer and in his fields, Naomi and Ruth were able to find food to survive. Read the following steps in the process of grain farming. Cut out the descriptions and arrange them on another sheet of paper in the order in which they would be done. Then cut out the pictures of each step and place each next to its description. Glue down the pictures and descriptions.

The good grain was stored in great earthenware pots.

WINNOWING

The farmer used a sickle, a sharp curved tool to cut the stalks. Only the top of the stalk was cut, leaving the rest of the plant for sheep to eat. Farmers were to leave the grain in the corners of the field for the poor people and widows like Naomi and Ruth. The farmer was also not allowed to go back over his field to collect any grain that was missed. This grain was also to be left for the needy

HARVEST

Threshing is beating or crushing the cut grain in order to separate it from the straw stems. The farmer used sticks to beat it or had his oxen trample it.

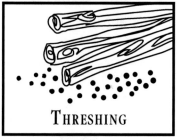
THRESHING

Once the grain was separated from the straw stems, the farmer would winnow it in order to further separate the grain from the bits of straw and husk (called chaff). Using a wooden winnowing fork, the farmer tossed the grain in the air. Chaff is light and is blown away by the wind. The heavier grain falls to the ground. Any bits of chaff are finally removed by shaking the grain in a sieve.

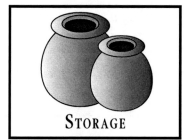
STORAGE

Plowing is the process of digging up the ground. In October and November rain would come and soften the dried earth. This made the plowing easier. Two donkeys or oxen pulled the plow that was a T-shaped tool with a sharp spike to cut through the ground. The farmer would frequently plow and sow at the same time. Sowing is scattering the seed. By sowing while plowing, the seed would be covered by dirt so that birds would not eat the seeds.

PLOWING & SOWING

NAOMI AND RUTH
Test

1. What is the Scripture reference and date for Naomi and Ruth?

   _____

   _____

2. How was Ruth related to Naomi?

   _____

   _____

3. From what nation was Ruth?

   _____

   _____

4. What did people call Naomi when she returned to Israel?

   _____

   _____

5. Whom did Ruth marry?

   _____

   _____

6. Decribe how Ruth got her new husband.

   _____

   _____

7. Who are the two most famous descendants of Ruth?

   _____

   _____

8. What is the law by which a close relative avenges enemies and cares for the survivors of those who had lost their husbands?

   _____

   _____

NAOMI AND RUTH
Test, Page 2

Review

1. List two specific sins of the Israelites in the time of the judges.

   _____

   _____

2. Describe how Eglon was killed.

   _____

   _____

3. Whom did Deborah summon to lead Israel in battle?

   _____

   _____

4. What sign did Gideon ask of God before he went into battle with the Midianites?

   _____

   _____

   _____

5. List all of the titles, Scripture references, and dates studied so far.

   _____

   _____

   _____

   _____

   _____

   _____

SAMSON AND DELILAH
Worksheet

1. What is the Scripture reference and date for Samson and Delilah?

   _____

   _____

2. From what nation did God deliver Israel by raising up Samson?

   _____

   _____

3. How was Samson's birth special?

   _____

   _____

   _____

4. Name two things that a Nazarite was not allowed to do.

   _____

   _____

   _____

   _____

5. What unusual "weapon" did Samson use to kill a thousand Philistines?

   _____

   _____

6. With what Philistine woman did Samson fall in love?

   _____

   _____

   _____

SAMSON AND DELILAH
Worksheet, Page 2

7. What was the secret of Samson's great strength?

_____

_____

_____

8. Describe how the Philistines finally captured Samson and tell what they did to him?

_____

_____

_____

_____

9. Describe Samson's death. (2 points)

_____

_____

_____

_____

_____

Samson and Delilah
Project 1—Bible Reading

There are several interesting stories from the life of Samson. Students are to read one or more of these stories in the passages suggested below. Then write a paragraph on each story read which explains what happened, including at least five details or facts not listed on the card. For teachers with multiple students it is suggested that the stories be divided among the students. When each student has completed his assignment, they can take turns reading their paragraphs to others.

Story Passages

Samson's Birth (Judges 13)
Samson and the Riddle (Judges 14)
Samson Kills Many Philistines (Judges 15)
Samson and Delilah (Judges 16:1–22)
Samson's Death (Judges 16:23–31)

_____
_____
_____
_____
_____
_____
_____
_____
_____
_____
_____
_____
_____

Samson and Delilah
Project 2—Judge Sorting

Each child will need six sheets of square paper (8" or 8.5" is a good size). Fold the paper in half to make a triangle. Hold the triangle with the long side toward you. Fold one "arm" (side point of the triangle) over so the point touches the opposite side of the triangle and the top line of the arm is parallel to the bottom (long) side of the big triangle.

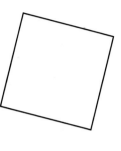

Fold the other arm over so that the point touches the opposite side of the triangle and the top line of the arm is also parallel to the bottom (long) side of the big triangle. Glue the top arm to the bottom arm. Then fold one top point of the triangle down so that the fold is along the top edges of the arms. Glue that top point down. Fold the remaining top point of the triangle backwards so that its fold is in line with the fold of the other top point. Glue that point down. This makes the project have an opening that can hold things. (Students will be interested to know that it can hold water, and they can drink from it like a cup.) Students will make a total of six of these pockets and glue them to a large sheet of paper.

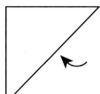
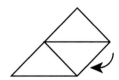

On the front of each pocket write the name of a judge: Othniel, Ehud, Deborah, Gideon, Jephthah, and Samson. Give each student page 2 of the project. Students cut out the clue and put that strip in the pocket with the label of the judge that matches the clue. The number of clues varies for each judge.

SAMSON AND DELILAH
Project 2, Page 2

Judges 3	made the Ephraimites say a word they could not pronounce
Judges 3	helped Barak defeat the Canaanites
Judges 4-5	told a riddle about a lion and honey at his wedding
Judges 6-7	tore down the altars of Baal at his Father's house at night.
Judges 11-12	
Judges 13-16	chased out of town by his brothers
was also a prophetess	tied the tails of foxes together and let them loose in the Philistine's fields
killed 1000 Philistines with a donkey's jawbone	asked God to make the fleece wet and the ground dry
was left-handed	gave his daughter two months to weep with her friends
vowed to sacrifice the first thing that came out of the house	killed more of God's enemies in his death by pushing down pillars that held up a building
was the first judge	
was a Nazarite	eyes were poked out
killed King Eglon	fought against Sisera
sent away those who were afraid and lapped water like a dog	the secret of his strength was to not cut his hair
prophesied that the glory of victory would go to a woman	his line died out
went into battle with only 300 men	mother wasn't able to have children without God's help
got in to see the king by saying he had a secret message from God	

SAMSON AND DELILAH
Project 3—Biblical Art Study

Rembrandt was born in Leiden on July 15, 1606. After attending a Latin school, Rembrandt began studying art when he was fourteen. He moved to Amsterdam to learn from the historical master Pieter Lastman. When he was 22, he started to teach art in Leiden. He moved to Amsterdam in 1631 and married Saskia in 1634. *The Blinding of Samson* is the epitome of Rembrandt's biblical works. The story of Samson, which was popular with the Baroque public, is prominent in Rembrandt's production during the 1630's. He painted *Samson Threatening his Father-in-Law* and the *Marriage of Samson*. His *Blinding of Samson*, more than any other work, shows Rembrandt's unrivalled use of the *chiaroscuro* (the use of extreme contrasts of lighting for dramatic effect) to appeal to his contemporaries' interest in the sensational. It is his most gruesome and violent work. By the time this painting was made he had long since abandoned conventional Dutch smoothness and his surfaces were already caked with paint. Though his palette was limited even by seventeenth century standards, Rembrandt was renowned as a colorist for he was able to maintain a balance between painting tonally, with light and shade, and painting in color.

Samson and Delilah
Project 3, Page 2

Using the artwork on the cover of this manual or the image on this sheet, discuss Rembrandt's The Blinding of Samson.

1. Who are the soldiers in the painting?

   _____

   _____

2. What appears to be the job of the man in the foreground holding the halberd (ax-like blade on a long shaft)? What is his "job" as part of the painting?

   _____

   _____

   _____

   _____

3. As Delilah rushes out of the tent, what emotions does she seem to be experiencing?

   _____

   _____

   _____

   _____

4. What things are out of place in the painting if the work is showing an event from the time of the Judges?

   _____

   _____

   _____

   _____

SAMSON AND DELILAH
Test

1. What is the Scripture reference and date for Samson and Delilah?

   _____

   _____

2. God called Samson to deliver Israel from what nation?

   _____

   _____

3. What did the angel tell Samson's mother?

   _____

   _____

   _____

4. Name two things that a Nazarite was not allowed to do.

   _____

   _____

   _____

   _____

5. What special ability did Samson have?

   _____

   _____

6. Describe one thing Samson did to bring judgment on the Philistines.

   _____

   _____

   _____

   _____

   _____

SAMSON AND DELILAH
Test, Page 2

7. Describe how the Philistines finally captured Samson and tell what they did to him.

_____

_____

_____

_____

8. Describe how Samson died.

_____

_____

_____

_____

Review

1. Who killed Eglon?

_____

_____

2. What was the consequence of Barak's hesitance to lead Israel in battle against Sisera?

_____

_____

_____

3. How did Gideon and the Israelites defeat the Midianites?

_____

_____

_____

_____

SAMSON AND DELILAH
Review, Page 3

4. What happened to Jephthah's line because of his vow?

_____

_____

_____

5. List all of the titles, Scripture references, and dates studied so far.

_____

_____

_____

_____

_____

_____

_____

HANNAH AND ELI
Worksheet

1. What is the Scripture reference and date for Hannah and Eli?

   _____

   _____

2. Why did Elkanah and his wives go up to Shiloh?

   _____

   _____

3. What was Hannah's problem? Who harassed her about the problem?

   _____

   _____

   _____

4. What wouldn't Hannah do because she was so upset by her problem?
   What did she do instead?

   _____

   _____

   _____

   _____

5. Who was Eli?

   _____

   _____

6. What vow did Hannah make?

   _____

   _____

   _____

"SHE CALLED HIS NAME SAMUEL."

HANNAH AND ELI
Worksheet, Page 2

7. What did Eli think was wrong with Hannah?

_____

_____

8. What was the name of the child born to Hannah?

_____

_____

9. When did Hannah fulfill her vow?

_____

_____

_____

HANNAH AND ELI
Project 1—Bible Reading

Read in I Samuel 1-2 about Hannah and Eli. Then complete the word find below and be sure to know what each word has to do with the story.

```
H A N N A A H E L K A N N A H V
E O W E A N E D N E D B U S T A
P V R D A L P H P S W O R D E L
T W A D H R A Z E R W E A N E O
W E A N E A C H I L O L E S S U
T S D R O N N R T Y U V O W I C
E A S E L I C N V B N M O P O H
L M B S L S C X A Z X C V K N I
K U V E S K V B N H G H J K E L
A E V P R S A W E R L G W D A D
N L E R A N S N S U K R O R M L
A P R E Z L A S A T J A R U O E
S A I S O E M C S H H C K N E S
D O T S R S A K L S Y E S K L S
G L A G U L F J W E P T F G H J
H N S H Y I G H B I B L E A B C
```

Hannah	wept	drunk
Elkanah	vow	Samuel
provoked	razor	weaned
childless	Eli	
tabernacle		

HANNAH AND ELI
Project 2—Clothespin Figures

Make clothespin figures of Hannah, Eli, Peninnah, and Baby Samuel to act out this story.

Materials

3 wooden clothespins per child

felt/fabric

pipe cleaners

small wiggly eyes

yarn/string

fine tip pen

glue

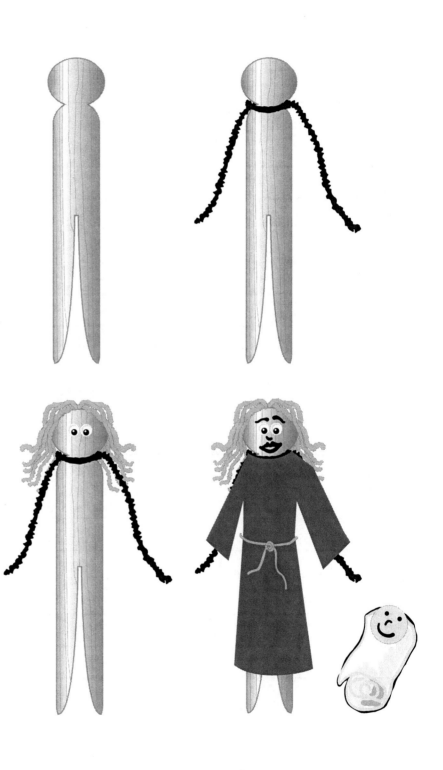

Wrap the center of 4" pipe cleaner around the "neck" of each clothespin once. Twist and bend the two ends of the pipe cleaner to make arms. Trim the ends to adjust the length if needed. Glue wiggly eyes to the "head" of each clothespin and glue yarn to make hair. Using a fine tip pen draw other facial features as desired. Cut clothes from the felt or fabric and glue them to the clothespins. Make a small bundle of cloth to be a swaddled baby Samuel. Cut a small circle of paper and draw a face on it. Glue this face of the end of the bundle of cloth. Now you have characters to act out the story of Hannah and Eli.

HANNAH AND ELI
Test

1. What is the Scripture reference and date for Hannah and Eli?

   _____

   _____

2. Who was Hannah's husband?

   _____

   _____

3. Who was Peninnah, and what did she do to Hannah?

   _____

   _____

   _____

4. Why did Hannah go to the tabernacle?

   _____

   _____

   _____

5. Who was Eli?

   _____

   _____

6. What did Hannah vow?

   _____

   _____

   _____

HANNAH AND ELI
Test, Page 2

7. What did Eli think was wrong with Hannah?

_____

_____

_____

8. Upon hearing Hannah's story, what did Eli tell her?

_____

_____

_____

9. How did God answer Hannah's prayer?

_____

_____

_____

Review

1. In addition to being a judge, what other job did Deborah have?

_____

_____

_____

2. Who killed Sisera?

_____

_____

3. Why did God have Gideon reduce the number of men that would go into battle?

_____

_____

4. What did Jephthah vow to God?

_____

_____

5. Who left grain for Ruth so that she and Naomi could survive?

_____

_____

6. List all of the titles, Scripture references, and dates studied so far.

_____

_____

_____

_____

_____

_____

_____

_____

SAMUEL, THE LAST JUDGE OF ISRAEL
Worksheet

1. What is the Scripture reference and date for Samuel, the Last Judge of Israel?

   _____

   _____

2. How had Hophni and Phinehas sinned?

   _____

   _____

   _____

   _____

3. Describe how God called Samuel.

   _____

   _____

   _____

   _____

   _____

   _____

4. What was the message that God gave to Samuel about Eli's family?

   _____

   _____

   _____

   _____

5. Samuel saw the rise and fall of _____ and he anointed

   _____ as king of Israel.

SAMUEL, THE LAST JUDGE OF ISRAEL
Project 1—Bible Reading

Read in I Samuel 2:12-3:21 about the corruption of Eli's family and Samuel's calling as a prophet and leader in Israel. Then answer the questions below.

How were priests supposed to take part of a sacrifice for themselves?

_____

_____

_____

How did Eli's sons take their share of a sacrifice?

_____

_____

_____

What did God say that Eli had done wrong? (I Samuel 3:13)

_____

_____

_____

When Samuel heard of God's judgment on Eli's house, how did he react? (I Samuel 3:15)

_____

_____

_____

What was Eli's reaction to what Samuel told him? (I Samuel 3:18)

_____

_____

_____

SAMUEL, THE LAST JUDGE OF ISRAEL
Project 2

Make a chart and/or bar graph showing the length of time in which the people were enslaved and freed during the time of some of the judges. Fill in the chart below first. Each box has the Scripture reference for where to find the information.

Years of Enslavement and Freedom During the Judges

JUDGE	ENSLAVEMENT	FREEDOM
Othniel	Judges 3:8 [ ] years	Judges 3:11 [ ] years
Ehud	Judges 3:14 [ ] years	Judges 3:30 [ ] years
Deborah	Judges 4:3 [ ] years	Judges 5:31 [ ] years
Gideon	Judges 6:1 [ ] years	Judges 8:28 [ ] years
Jephthah	Judges 10:8 [ ] years	Judges 12:7 [ ] years
Samson	Judges 13:1 [ ] years	Judges 15:20 [ ] years

SAMUEL, THE LAST JUDGE OF ISRAEL
Project 2, Page 2

Now use the same information to complete the bar graph. The bars of Othniel are drawn for you. Color all the bars showing years of enslavement in one color. Color all the bars showing years of freedom in a different color.

Years of Enslavement and Freedom During the Judges

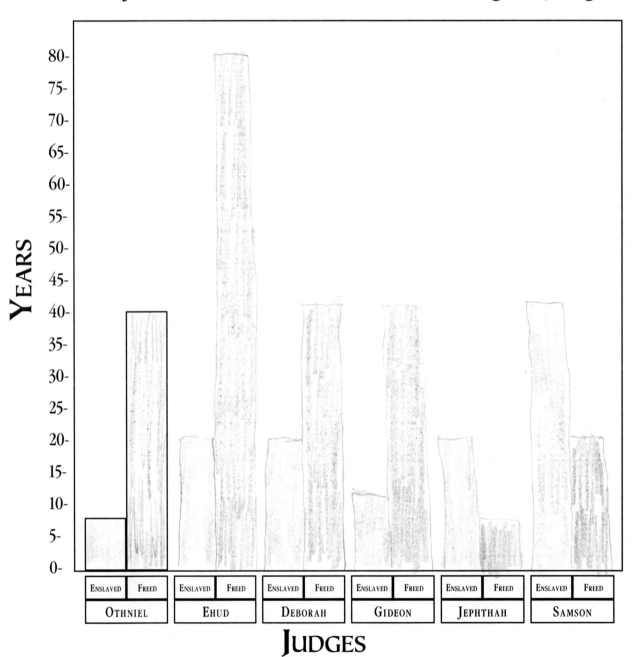

SAMUEL, THE LAST JUDGE OF ISRAEL
Project 2, Page 3

This graph puts this information in chronological order from left to right. Look at the graph keeping in mind God's sovereignty over the years Israel was enslaved and freed. Also consider as you move toward the right on the graph how many times Israel had forsaken the Lord and been delivered by Him over and over again.

1. What do you notice about the length of their enslavement as the cycle of faithlessness, repentance, and deliverance repeated time and time again?

_____

_____

_____

_____

2. What do you notice about the length of their freedom as the cycle was repeated over and over again?

_____

_____

_____

_____

3. What do you notice about the difference between the lengths of their enslavement and freedom as the cycle is repeated over time?

_____

_____

_____

_____

SAMUEL, THE LAST JUDGE OF ISRAEL
Test

1. What is the Scripture reference and date for Samuel, the Last Judge of Israel?

    _____

    _____

2. What were the names of Eli's two sons?

    _____

    _____

3. Name three ways in which Eli's sons sinned.

    _____

    _____

    _____

4. What woke up Samuel in the middle of the night? Who did Samuel think that this was?

    _____

    _____

    _____

5. How many times was Samuel awakened before Eli realized who was actually calling Samuel?

    _____

    _____

6. What was the message that God gave to Samuel?

    _____

    _____

    _____

7. Name one thing Samuel saw or did during his days as a judge.

    _____

    _____

SAMUEL, THE LAST JUDGE OF ISRAEL
Test, Page 2

Review

1. Who was the first judge?

   _____

   _____

2. How did Barak respond to Deborah when she asked him to lead Israel in battle?

   _____

   _____

3. Describe one way in which Gideon narrowed down his troops.

   _____

   _____

   _____

4. What was the first thing that came out of Jephthah's house when he returned from battle?

   _____

   _____

   _____

5. Whom did Boaz have to talk to before he could possibly marry Ruth?

   _____

   _____

   _____

6. List all of the titles, Scripture references, and dates studied so far.

   _____

   _____

   _____

   _____

SAMUEL, THE LAST JUDGE OF ISRAEL
Test, Page 3

6. (continued)

_____

_____

_____

_____

_____

_____

THE ARK IS TAKEN INTO CAPTIVITY
Worksheet

1. What is the Scripture reference and date for the Ark is Taken Into Captivity?

   _____

   _____

2. Why did the Israelites take the Ark into battle?

   _____

   _____

   _____

3. Name two results of the battle on the day that the Ark was taken along.

   _____

   _____

   _____

   _____

4. How did Eli die?

   _____

   _____

   _____

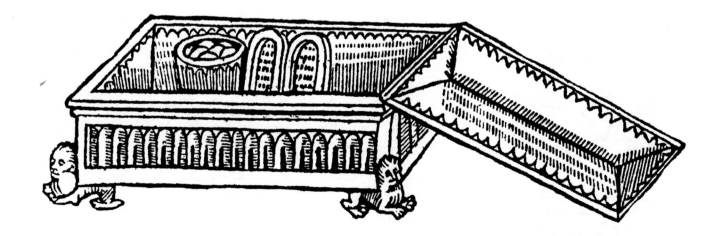

THE ARK IS TAKEN INTO CAPTIVITY
Worksheet, Page 2

5. Who captured the Ark?

_____

_____

_____

6. Where did they keep the Ark at first? What happened while the Ark was there?

_____

_____

_____

7. What happened in the cities where the Ark was kept?

_____

_____

_____

_____

8. Describe how they sent the Ark back to Israel.

_____

_____

_____

_____

_____

_____

_____

_____

_____

DAGON, THE FISH-GOD.

THE ARK IS TAKEN INTO CAPTIVITY
Project 1—Bible Reading

Read in I Samuel 4-6 about the Ark being taken into captivity. Look at the phrases and sentences below. Decide which part of speech each word is and then write it under the proper heading.

Philistines captured the Ark
Wicked Hophni died.
Dagon fell backwards.
five golden tumors
finally hitched a cart
two milk cows

Nouns   *Verbs*   *Adjectives*

_____   _____   _____

_____   _____   _____

_____   _____   _____

_____   _____   _____

_____   _____   _____

_____

Adverbs   *Articles*

_____   _____

_____   _____

THE ARK IS TAKEN INTO CAPTIVITY
Project 2

Strange things have been happening to the Philistines ever since they captured Israel's Ark of the Covenant—strange and terrible things! Now many Philistines want to get rid of the Ark. Write a letter to the editor of the Philistine Gazette voicing your desire (you are to write as a Philistine) to send the Ark back. Be sure to describe the trouble caused by the Ark.

THE ARK IS TAKEN INTO CAPTIVITY
Project 3

Cut out the following statements and arrange them in the order in which they occurred. Glue them to a large sheet of paper in the proper order. Fill in any blanks.

Eli fell over _____ and died.

God sent plagues of _____ and _____ on the cities where the Ark was kept.

The Israelites took the _____ into battle because they thought God would give them victory.

Dagon was found lying _____ before the Ark.

The _____ pulled the cart with the Ark straight back to Israel.

The Philistines put the Ark in the temple of their god _____.

_____ and _____ were killed and the Ark was _____.

They set Dagon back up.

The Philistines moved the Ark out of the temple of _____ and into another city.

The _____ defeated the Israelites in battle on the first two days.

The Ark was put on a _____ and hitched to _____.

Dagon was lying before the Ark with its _____ and _____ broken off.

THE ARK IS TAKEN INTO CAPTIVITY
Test

1. What is the Scripture reference and date for the Ark is Taken Into Captivity?

   _____

   _____

2. Who died in the battle on the day that the Ark was captured?

   _____

   _____

   _____

3. Who captured the Ark?

   _____

   _____

   _____

   _____

4. Describe Eli's death.

   _____

   _____

   _____

   _____

5. What happened while the Ark was in Dagon's temple?

   _____

   _____

   _____

   _____

THE ARK IS TAKEN INTO CAPTIVITY
Test, Page 2

6. What happened in the cities where the Ark was kept which made them want to send back the Ark?

_____

_____

_____

7. How was the Ark sent back to Israel.

_____

_____

_____

_____

Review

1. Who was the fat king that Ehud killed?

_____

_____

2. Which judge prophesied that the glory of defeating the enemy would go to a woman?

_____

_____

3. What does a kinsman-redeemer do?

_____

_____

4. What was the name of the child born to Hannah?

_____

_____

THE ARK IS TAKEN INTO CAPTIVITY
Test, Page 3

5. Describe how God called Samuel.

_____

_____

_____

_____

6. List all of the titles, Scripture references, and dates studied so far.

_____

_____

_____

_____

_____

_____

_____

_____

_____

_____

SAUL, THE FIRST KING OF ISRAEL
Worksheet

1. What is the Scripture reference and date for Saul, the First King of Israel?

   _____

   _____

2. Who was anointed as judges when Samuel grew old?

   _____

   _____

3. What kind of people were the new judges? Include one point of proof.

   _____

   _____

   _____

   _____

4. How did the people react to the new judges?

   _____

   _____

   _____

5. About what did God have Samuel warn the people?

   _____

   _____

   _____

   _____

6. Who was Israel's first king?

   _____

   _____

Samuel
anointing Saul.

SAUL, THE FIRST KING OF ISRAEL
Worksheet, Page 2

7. Why did Saul go to Samuel?

_____

_____

_____

8. Describe how Samuel announced to the people who would be king.

_____

_____

_____

9. Where was Saul when the announcement was made to the people?

_____

_____

SAUL, THE FIRST KING OF ISRAEL
Project 1—Bible Reading

Read about Saul being anointed as the first king of Israel in I Samuel 9, 10. Then complete the following statements. Use the number of blanks and letter clues to help you.

1. Saul was from the tribe of _ e _ _ _ _ _ _.

2. Saul was a _ _ _ _ s _ _ _ man.

3. Saul was looking for his _ _ t _ _ _' donkeys.

4. He only had one-fourth of a _ _ _ _ _ l of silver to pay Samuel.

5. Saul found Samuel on his way to make a s_ _ _ _ _ _ _ _ at a h_ _h _ _ _ _ _.

6. Samuel took a _l_ _ _ of oil and anointed Saul.

7. Saul met a group of p_ _p_ _ _ _ and God enabled him to prophesy.

8. When Saul was announced as king he was hiding behind the _ _ _ _ _ _ _.

9. Samuel wrote a book explaining the behavior of _ _ y _ _ _ y.

SAUL, THE FIRST KING OF ISRAEL
Project 2

Begin writing a diary for Saul to trace the events of his unique life. Photocopy on front and back at least 3 of the entry pages (found on the next page). For each event in Saul's life you will write an entry in his diary from his perspective. This means you should not include things in the entry about which Saul would not have known. Each entry should cover 2 sides of entry pages. If your entries are longer you will need to add extra entry pages to the back of your diary.

Place all three entry pages in a pile and fold them in half together. Keep the pages together as you work on the project. Also do not write close to the fold as that area will become part of the binding.

This is an ongoing project. Teachers should check the student's work after each entry and either store the project until the next time or guide the students in how to safely hold on to their work. The diary will be added to during the study of the following cards:

Saul, the First King of Israel (Card 43)

Saul's Sin at Amalek (Card 45)

David is Anointed as King (Card 46)

David and Goliath (Card 47)

Jonathan Protects David (Card 48)

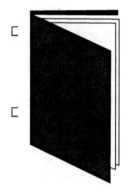

When all entries are completed, cut a construction paper cover a little larger than the entry page. Assemble the entry pages in order and fold the cover around them. Staple close to the fold to secure the cover and pages. The cover may be decorated. Some students may wish to design a special closing or lock for the diary.

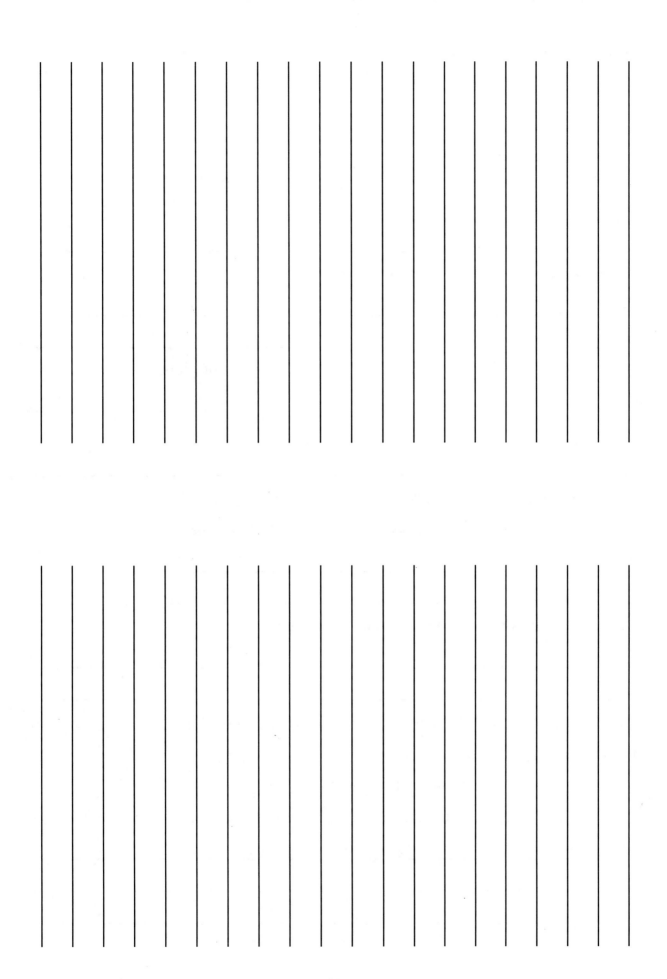

SAUL, THE FIRST KING OF ISRAEL
Test

1. What is the Scripture reference and date for Saul, the First King of Israel?

   _____

   _____

2. Who was anointed as judges when Samuel grew old?

   _____

   _____

3. What kind of people were the new judges? Include one point of proof.

   _____

   _____

   _____

4. Israel wanted a king so they could be like _____.

5. Name two things that Samuel warned the people that a king would do.

   _____

   _____

6. What was Saul looking for when he went to Samuel?

   _____

   _____

7. When Samuel announced the new king he gathered together _____

   and then narrowed it down by _____, _____, and

   _____ until he finally came to _____.

8. Where was Saul when the announcement was made to the people?

   _____

   _____

   _____

SAUL, THE FIRST KING OF ISRAEL
Test, Page 2

Review

1. What did God do for his people when they cried out to him because of the oppression they were suffering?

   _____

   _____

   _____

2. How was Naomi related to Ruth?

   _____

   _____

   _____

3. How was Samson's birth special?

   _____

   _____

   _____

   _____

4. How did Samson die?

   _____

   _____

   _____

   _____

5. Who harassed Hannah about her problem?

   _____

   _____

   _____

SAUL, THE FIRST KING OF ISRAEL
Test, Page 3

6. What was the message that God gave to Samuel about Eli's family?

_____

_____

_____

_____

7. List all of the titles, Scripture references, and dates studied so far.

_____

_____

_____

_____

_____

_____

_____

_____

_____

_____

_____

THE GENEALOGY OF DAVID
Worksheet

1. What is the Scripture reference and date for the Genealogy of David?

   _____

   _____

2. Fill in the blanks.

   _____

   _____

   _____

   _____

   Perez

   Hezron

   Ram

   Amminadab

   Nahshon

   Salmon

   _____

   _____

   _____

   _____

3. Who was called the father of the nation of Israel?

   _____

   _____

4. How was Isaac's birth special?

   _____

   _____

THE GENEALOGY OF DAVID
Worksheet, Page 2

5. What was God showing about himself with Isaac's special birth?

_____

_____

_____

6. What did Jacob's sons become?

_____

_____

7. What was the reputation of the tribe of Judah?

_____

_____

_____

8. Who married Ruth?

_____

_____

9. Who was the son of Ruth?

_____

_____

10. How many sons did Jesse have?

_____

_____

11. Who was Jesse's youngest son?

_____

_____

THE GENEALOGY OF DAVID
Project 1—Bible Reading

Read David's genealogy in I Chronicles 2. Then fill in the tree showing Judah's descendants. The first letter of each name is given to help you.

Looking at this project, you can see several things about big genealogies. For one thing, they are usually not a complete listings of all descendants. This genealogy emphasizes the line from Judah to David. The author chose to list some people for their righteousness or sinfulness. This genealogy only names seven sons of Jesse and Elihu was skipped—possibly because he didn't have any children.

If you read the genealogy in Matthew 1, you will see that line has a different emphasis and omits and includes different people.

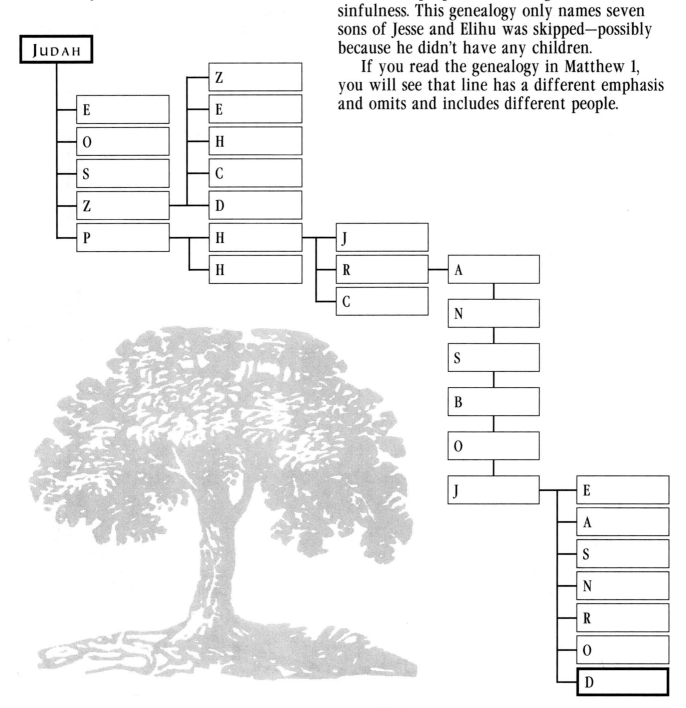

THE GENEALOGY OF DAVID
Project 2

It was an ancient practice to have a special banner or standard to represent a nation, tribe, or family. A coat of arms is a similar combination of symbols and patterns to represent who a person is and who his ancestors were. Each generation the coat of arms would change, adding in new symbols, some depicting symbols for a child's father and mother's ancestors. *Design a coat of arms for David using at least three symbols or objects which relate to his ancestors. Remember that numbers were important. Do you remember what God told Abraham his descendants would be like? Use your Bible and other resources to recall events from the lives of these ancestors which might give you ideas for symbols. You may even find what animal was a symbol for the tribe of Judah.*

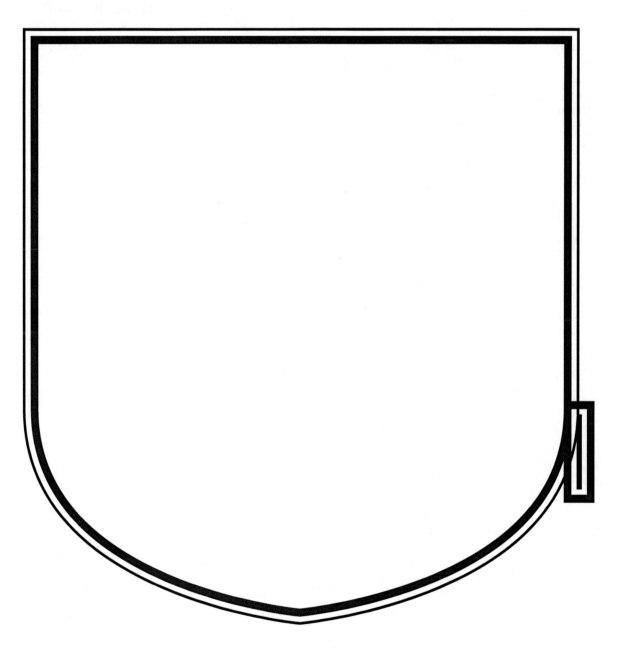

THE GENEALOGY OF DAVID
Test

1. What is the Scripture reference and date for the Genealogy of David?

    _____

    _____

2. Fill in the blanks.

    _____

    _____

    _____

    Perez

    Hezron

    Ram

    Amminadab

    Nahshon

    Salmon

    _____

    _____

    _____

3. Which tribe had the reputation for being the strongest militarily and spiritually?

    _____

    _____

4. Who was Ruth's husband?

    _____

    _____

THE GENEALOGY OF DAVID
Test, Page 2

5. What did Jacob's sons become?

_____

_____

6. Who was the father of Israel?

_____

_____

7. Who was Jesse's youngest son?

_____

_____

8. Who was Ruth's son?

_____

_____

9. How many sons did Jesse have?

_____

_____

10. How was Isaac's birth special?

_____

_____

_____

Review

1. Who is the most famous person that descended from Ruth?

_____

_____

THE GENEALOGY OF DAVID
Test, Page 3

2. Fill in the blanks to show the pattern of Judges.

   The Israelites sin by _____

   God punishes Israel by _____

   The Israelites finally _____

   God sends a _____

   The people are _____

   But then the Israelites _____

3. List all of the titles, Scripture references, and dates studied so far.

   _____

   _____

   _____

   _____

   _____

   _____

   _____

   _____

   _____

   _____

   _____

   _____

   _____

Saul's Sin at Amalek
Worksheet

1. What is the Scripture reference and date for Saul's Sin at Amalek?

   _____

   _____

2. God commanded Saul to kill every _____ and every

   _____ of the Amalekites.

3. Name two ways in which Saul did not follow the Lord's command.

   _____

   _____

   _____

   _____

4. How did Saul greet Samuel after the battle with the Amalekites?

   _____

   _____

   _____

5. Whom did Saul blame for the disobedience concerning the animals?

   _____

   _____

   _____

6. What did Saul say they intended to do with the animals?

   _____

   _____

   _____

SAUL'S SIN AT AMALEK
Worksheet, Page 2

7. Who was Agag?

   _____

   _____

8. What was the punishment for Saul's sin at Amalek?

   _____

   _____

   _____

9. Saul had previously sinned by not waiting for Samuel to_____

   _____.

SAUL'S SIN AT AMALEK
Project 1—Bible Reading

Read in I Samuel 15 about Saul's sin at Amalek. Then fill in the text and crossword puzzle below.

God commanded Saul to _____ all of the _____.
                       (1 down)   (2 across)

But Saul_____ King _____ and the best of the cattle and
              (3 across)   (2 down)

_____The prophet _____ was sent by God, and he
        (4 down)   (5 down)

asked Saul about the _____that was kept by the Israelites.
                       (6 across)

Saul _____ the people and said they were going to_____ the animals.
        (7 across)   (8 across)

Because Saul _____ God's command he was _____
          (1 across)   (9 down)

as king. Samuel _____ King Agag to pieces.
               (10 down)

SAUL'S SIN AT AMALEK
Project 2—Comic Strip

Draw a comic strip illustrating this story. Your comic strip must contain at least four scenes. Use dialog bubbles to include important things that were said.

Saul's Sin at Amalek
Test

1. What is the Scripture reference and date for Saul's Sin at Amalek?

   _____

   _____

2. What command did God have Samuel give to Saul concerning the Amalekites?

   _____

   _____

3. Name two ways in which Saul did not follow the Lord's command.

   _____

   _____

   _____

4. Whom did Saul blame for the disobedience concerning the animals?

   _____

   _____

5. What did Saul say they intended to do with the animals?

   _____

   _____

6. Who was the king of Amalek?

   _____

   _____

SAUL'S SIN AT AMALEK
Test, Page 2

7. What was the punishment for Saul's sin at Amalek?

_____

_____

_____

8. What other serious sin had Saul committed before this sin at Amalek?

_____

_____

_____

_____

Review

1. What were the Israelites to do to the Canaanites living in the Promised Land?

_____

_____

_____

2. What does the name Mara mean? Who was given the name of Mara?

_____

_____

_____

3. With what Philistine woman did Samson fall in love?

_____

_____

4. How did Eli die?

_____

_____

_____

_____

5. Describe how Samuel announced to the people who would be king.

_____

_____

_____

_____

6. List all of the titles, Scripture references, and dates studied so far.

_____

_____

_____

_____

_____

_____

_____

_____

_____

_____

_____

_____

DAVID IS ANOINTED AS KING
Worksheet

1. What is the Scripture reference and date for David is Anointed as King?

   _____

   _____

2. What information does God give Samuel about the person that will be king?

   _____

   _____

3. What does Samuel do in order to keep Saul from becoming angry at him?

   _____

   _____

4. Why does Samuel think that Eliab will be the new king?

   _____

   _____

   _____

5. When Samuel sees the seven sons of Jesse, what question does he ask?

   _____

   _____

   _____

6. Where was Jesse's youngest son?

   _____

   _____

   _____

DAVID IS ANOINTED AS KING
Worksheet, Page 2

7. Name two things that God does to Saul after he anoints David.

_____

_____

_____

_____

8. What do his servants suggest to Saul to help with his problem?

_____

_____

_____

9. Who was chosen to serve Saul in this way?

_____

_____

10. What special honor does Saul give to David?

_____

_____

_____

DAVID IS ANOINTED AS KING
Project 1—Bible Reading

Read about David's anointing as the next king in I Samuel 16. Unscramble the words from the story. Each word matches a phrase on the right so if you get stuck on a scrambled word try to come up with possible words that fit the phrases below. Draw a line connecting each scrambled word with its matching phrase.

feirhe   1. tending _____

prah   2. the spirit would _____

norh   3. a _____ to sacrifice

rabermoaarer   4. looks at the _____

hater   5. _____ player

traped   6. _____ spirit

epesh   7. _____ with oil

niterdsssig   8. became his _____

DAVID IS ANOINTED AS KING
Project 2—David the Shepherd

When Samuel came to anoint the next king of Israel, David was out tending the sheep. The following statements below tell about David's experience as a shepherd. Read over the statements. Then read Psalm 23, which was written by David. If you see a connection between a verse in the Psalm and one of the statements about a shepherd, write the verse number in the blank next to the statement. Not every statement has a connection to a verse in Psalm 23. Jesus is the Good Shepherd of which David is writing. You may wish to look at the statements below and see the connections to what Jesus said in John 10:14–16, 25–30.

1. Shepherds carried a club or rod, a sling, and a staff to defend the sheep from wild animals. _____

2. The sheep knew the voice of their shepherd. _____

3. In the summer, the grass near the village dried up, so the shepherd had to take his flock away to find pasture. _____

4. A shepherd's staff was helpful to him when walking in rough country.

   _____

5. A shepherd tended sheep and goats in the same flock. _____

6. A shepherd had to find a good water supply for his flock. _____

7. At night sheep were kept in a sheepfold or cave. _____

8. A good shepherd leads his sheep; he does not drive them. They will follow him as he walks. _____

9. A shepherd sometimes watched after all of the sheep in the village. _____

10. Sheep are helpless animals. The shepherd had to provide for their every need. _____

11. A shepherd carried his food in a leather bag called a scrip. _____

DAVID IS ANOINTED AS KING
Test

1. What is the Scripture reference and date for David is Anointed as King?

   _____

   _____

2. Who did God tell Samuel was the father of the man he was to anoint as king?

   _____

   _____

   _____

3. Why did Samuel go to make a sacrifice when he anointed the new king?

   _____

   _____

   _____

4. Describe Eliab.

   _____

   _____

   _____

   _____

5. Where was David?

   _____

   _____

6. Describe David's appearance.

   _____

   _____

   _____

   _____

DAVID IS ANOINTED AS KING
Test, Page 2

7. Name two things that God does to Saul after he anoints David.

   _____

   _____

   _____

   _____

8. What do his servants suggest to Saul to help with his problem?

   _____

   _____

   _____

9. What special honor does Saul give to David?

   _____

   _____

   _____

Review

1. What happened to Jephthah's daughter?

   _____

   _____

   _____

2. What did Ruth do to make Boaz decide that he wanted to marry her?

   _____

   _____

   _____

DAVID IS ANOINTED AS KING
Test, Page 3

3. What vow did Hannah make?

_____

_____

4. Who were Hophni and Phinehas?

_____

_____

5. Where was Saul when it was announced that he would be king of Israel?

_____

_____

_____

6. . List all of the titles, Scripture references, and dates studied so far.

_____

_____

_____

_____

_____

_____

_____

_____

_____

_____

_____

_____

DAVID AND GOLIATH
Worksheet

1. What is the Scripture reference and date for David and Goliath?

   _____

   _____

2. What was the challenge that Goliath made?

   _____

   _____

   _____

   _____

3. How many days did Goliath come forward to make his challenge?

   _____

   _____

4. From what country was Goliath?

   _____

   _____

5. Who finally accepted Goliath's challenge?

   _____

   _____

6. Why was David angry at Goliath?

   _____

   _____

   _____

7. What did Saul give David?

   _____

   _____

DAVID AND GOLIATH
Worksheet, Page 2

8. How useful was Saul's gift?

_____

_____

_____

9. What weapons did David use to kill Goliath?

_____

_____

_____

_____

DAVID AND GOLIATH
Project 1—Bible Reading

Read in I Samuel 17 about David and Goliath. Then write a sentence using the following phrases as they are used in the story.

1. 5,000 shekels

   _____

   _____

2. one champion

   _____

   _____

3. forty days

   _____

   _____

4. three sons

   _____

   _____

5. ten cheeses

   _____

   _____

6. five stones

   _____

   _____

7. no sword

   _____

   _____

DAVID AND GOLIATH
Project 2—Biblical Art Study

Michelangelo Merisi (1571-1610), an Italian painter, was named for the town he grew up in—Caravaggio. He was trained in Milan, then in 1593 he was in Rome working for other painters and getting in trouble with the police. Around 1596 things changed for Caravaggio when he was commissioned to paint a series of large paintings for a chapel.

Caravaggio was a talented artist but had difficulties staying out of trouble. His artwork was often violently criticized by the clergy, and he continued getting into fights. During one brawl at the pinaccle of his success as a painter, Caravaggio killed a man in a deal that set off a large melee, and so he had to flee Rome. His final years consisted of short periods spent painting at Naples, Malta and Sicily (Caravaggio left each city after he had, again, started a fight).

As an artist he painted directly from the low life models. His best innovation was a technique called *chiaroscuro* (the use of extreme contrasts of lighting for dramatic effect). The imitation of his work inspired a school of painting in Spain, the Caravaggisti, and years later his art directly affected the work of Rembrandt.

Using the artwork on the cover of this manual or the image on this sheet, discuss Caravaggio's David with the Head of Goliath.

1. Does this painting show that David killed Goliath at night?

_____

_____

2. How does Caravaggio show who is the morally superior character in the painting?

_____

_____

3. Comparing this painting and the one on the flashcard with the Scripture (I Sam. 16:18), which shows David's age more accurately?

_____

_____

DAVID AND GOLIATH
Project 3—Slingshot

How to Make a Sling

There are many materials you could use to make this sling—from paper and string to leather. For the best sling, cut the shape shown to the right out of a piece of leather and tie a piece of leather cord 1.5' long through the holes on either side. In the far end of one leather cord tie a knot. In the far end of the other leather cord tie a small loop as shown below. You are now prepared to line up empty soda cans and milk cartons in an open field then shout at the top of your lungs:

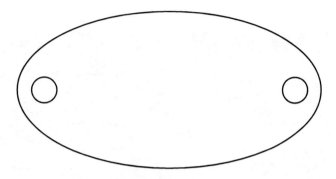

"I come to you in the name of the LORD of hosts, the God of the armies of Israel, whom you have defied. This day the LORD will deliver you into my hand, and I will strike you and take your head from you. And this day I will give the carcasses of the camp of the Philistines to the birds of the air and the wild beasts of the earth, that all the earth may know that there is a God in Israel."

Or something like that . . . and then start swinging!

How to Swing a Sling

The cord with the loop on the end is placed around the middle finger with cord trailing away from the back of your hand. The knotted cord is then held between the index finger and thumb. While holding the sling this way, let the pouch fall suspended. Load the projectile in the center of the dangling pouch. Projectiles can take many forms: mashmallows, foam balls, raquetballs, paintballs, and rocks. It all depends on how far you want to sling the object and how much damage you would like to inflict on your target. Remember, David *killed* a giant with one of these. Be careful and don't ever aim in the direction of another person.

After loading the sling as described above, swing the sling *forward* as in fast-pitch softball. Your arm should be moving at the shoulder, not at the wrist—making a large, somewhat diagonal circle in the air. Practice releasing your thumb at the moment when the projectile will leave at a 45 degree angle.

Or, for better accuracy with less power, start as before—underhanded and forward. As the sling is swinging, bring it over your head, your arm turning more at the elbow than the shoulder. The circle over your head should be about perpendicular with your body. Then throw your arm like you would if you were throwing a baseball but only when the pouch is swinging forward. Practice to get a feel for the release point.

DAVID AND GOLIATH
Test

1. What is the Scripture reference and date for David and Goliath?

   _____

   _____

2. What country was encamped across the valley from the Israelite army?

   _____

   _____

3. What was the challenge that Goliath made?

   _____

   _____

   _____

4. How many days did Goliath come forward to make his challenge?

   _____

   _____

5. What was David taking to his brothers when he found out about Goliath's challenge?

   _____

   _____

   _____

6. What fighting experience did David relate to Saul when he told Saul he would fight Goliath?

   _____

   _____

   _____

DAVID AND GOLIATH
Test, Page 2

7. What did Saul give David?

    _____

    _____

    _____

8. Why couldn't David use Saul's gift?

    _____

    _____

    _____

9. How was Goliath killed?

    _____

    _____

    _____

    _____

    _____

    _____

Review

1. How did God use a fleece to confirm that he was calling Gideon to lead Israel into battle?

    _____

    _____

    _____

2. What was the secret of Samson's great strength?

    _____

    _____

    _____

DAVID AND GOLIATH
Test, Page 3

3. Name one way in which Hophni and Phinehas sinned.

_____

_____

_____

4. Describe how the Philistines sent the Ark back to Israel.

_____

_____

_____

_____

DAVID AND GOLIATH
Test, Page 4

5. What kind of judges were Samuel's sons?

_____

_____

6. Whom did Saul blame for the disobedience concerning the animals?

_____

_____

7. List all of the titles, Scripture references, and dates studied so far.

_____

_____

_____

_____

_____

_____

_____

_____

_____

_____

_____

_____

_____

JONATHAN PROTECTS DAVID
Worksheet

1. What is the Scripture reference and date for Jonathan Protects David?

   _____

   _____

2. Why did David become so popular?

   _____

   _____

   _____

3. Why did Saul want to kill David?

   _____

   _____

   _____

4. How was Jonathan related to Saul?

   _____

   _____

   _____

5. Describe the relationship between
   Jonathan and David.

   _____

   _____

   _____

6. Why was it necessary to come up with the plan?

   _____

   _____

   _____

JONATHAN PROTECTS DAVID
Worksheet, Page 2

7. During what festival did Jonathan carry out his plan to inform David of Saul's intentions?

_____

_____

_____

8. Describe the plan that Jonathan and David had.

_____

_____

_____

_____

9. When the plan was carried out, what did David know he should do?

_____

_____

_____

_____

Jonathan Protects David
Project 1—Bible Reading

Read I Samuel 20. Then illustrate the two scenes described below. Use conversation bubbles to include the important things that were said.

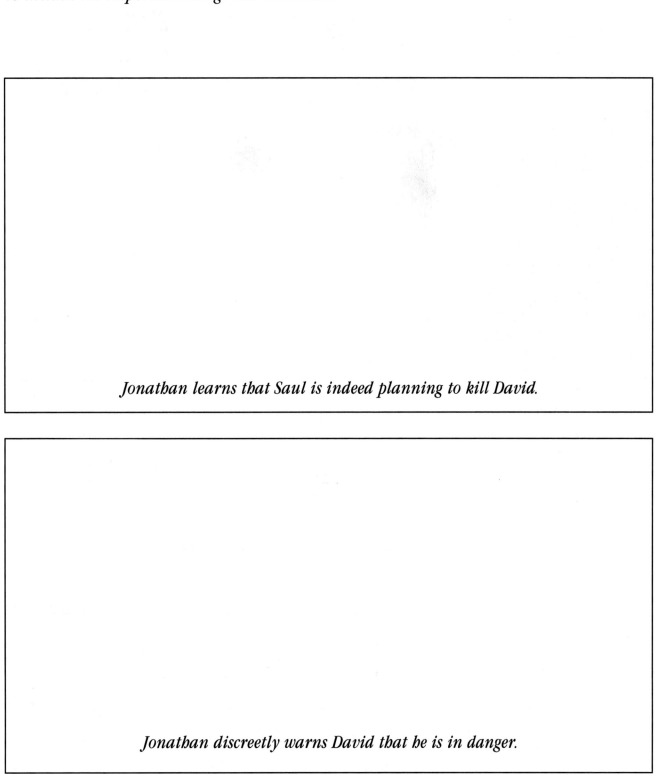

Jonathan learns that Saul is indeed planning to kill David.

Jonathan discreetly warns David that he is in danger.

Jonathan Protects David
Project 2—Missing Person Poster

David was on the run, and Saul was after him. Nowadays, police or other officials that are searching for someone may post a missing person poster or a wanted poster. Pretend you work for King Saul, and he has asked you to head up a search for David. Make a wanted poster including the following information: Name of person, physical description, who wants him, description of any reward offered, and any other information that might help people locate him. Draw a large portrait of David. Put the written information at the bottom of the poster.

JONATHAN PROTECTS DAVID
Test

1. What is the Scripture reference and date for Jonathan Protects David?

   _____

   _____

2. What event made David become so popular?

   _____

   _____

   _____

3. Why did Saul want to kill David?

   _____

   _____

   _____

4. How was Jonathan related to Saul?

   _____

   _____

   _____

5. Describe the relationship between Jonathan and David.

   _____

   _____

   _____

   _____

JONATHAN PROTECTS DAVID
Test, Page 2

6. What message was Jonathan trying to get to David at the new moon festival?

_____

_____

_____

_____

7. What did Jonathan pretend to be doing? Where was David while Jonathan was doing this?

_____

_____

_____

_____

8. By calling to the boy that the _____ were behind him,

Jonathan let David know _____

_____.

Review

1. How did Jephthah and the Gileadites test to identify any Ephraimites that were trying to escape after the battle?

_____

_____

_____

_____

JONATHAN PROTECTS DAVID
Test, Page 3

2. What did Eli think was wrong with Hannah when she was praying at the tabernacle?

_____

_____

_____

3. What did Samuel warn the people that a king would do?

_____

_____

_____

4. Describe how Samuel announced to the people who would be king.

_____

_____

_____

_____

5. What did Jacob's sons become?

_____

_____

_____

6. What was the punishment for Saul's sin at Amalek?

_____

_____

_____

JONATHAN PROTECTS DAVID
Test, Page 4

7. List all of the titles, Scripture references, and dates studied so far.

_____

_____

_____

_____

_____

_____

_____

_____

_____

_____

_____

_____

THE DEATHS OF SAUL AND JONATHAN
Worksheet

1. What is the Scripture reference and date for the Deaths of Saul and Jonathan?

   _____

   _____

2. Why wouldn't David kill Saul, even though Saul was trying to kill him?

   _____

   _____

   _____

3. Where was David living while it was unsafe for him in Israel?

   _____

   _____

4. How was Saul wounded?

   _____

   _____

   _____

5. What did Saul ask of his armor-bearer?

   _____

   _____

6. How did Saul die?

   _____

   _____

THE DEATHS OF SAUL AND JONATHAN
Worksheet, Page 2

7. Who else died with Saul in the battle?

_____

_____

_____

8.. What happened to the soldier who claimed to have killed Saul?

_____

_____

_____

_____

_____

9. What was the song written by David to mourn the deaths of Saul and Jonathan?

_____

_____

_____

_____

_____

THE DEATH OF SAUL AND JONATHAN
Project 1—Bible Reading

Despite the fact that Saul was trying to kill him (and David knew that God had chosen him to be king), David honored Saul and dealt with him righteously. Read I Samuel 26, 31, and II Samuel 1. Then write at least two sentences describing each of three ways in which David was loyal and honoring to a king that had tried to kill him.

1. _____
_____
_____
_____
_____
_____

2. _____
_____
_____
_____
_____
_____

3. _____
_____
_____
_____
_____
_____

THE DEATH OF SAUL AND JONATHAN
Project 2—Philistine Headdress

Saul and Jonathan were both killed in a battle against the Philistines. The Philistines had long been in conflict with the Israelites. In battle it would have been easy to determine which were the Philistine enemy by the unique headdresses that they wore. Make a headdress like those worn by the Philistines following the directions below.

Materials

Long strips of oaktag or lightweight cardboard (at least as long as the circumference of the student's head)

Metallic spray paint

Long feathers of the same color

Metal brad

Hole punch

Markers

Scissors

Glue (Hot glue works well)

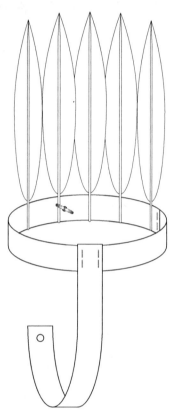

Directions

Cut a strip of oaktag 1 1/2 " wide and about one inch longer than the circumference of the student's head. Place the strip around the student's head to form a band. Hold the overlap on the band and remove the band. Staple the ends of the band where they overlap. Cut a second strip one inch wide and twenty inches long. Staple one end of the strip to the headband. Put the headband back on the student's head with the attached strip right in front of one ear. Pull the strip under the student's jaw and up to reach the top of the headband. Trim the strip to that length to make a chin strap. Punch a hole in the end of the loose chinstrap. With a pencil, put a small mark through the hole on the headband. Remove the headband and place a metal brad through the mark on the headband. Now the headband can be placed on the student's head and the chinstrap can be pulled under his chin and hooked on the metal brad. With spray paint and markers the headdress can be decorated. Glue feathers close together with the quills to the headband all the way around the headband (diagram is incomplete). You may wish to attach another strip of oaktag on the inside of the quills. This "inner headband" will provide more support, durability, and comfort.

THE DEATHS OF SAUL AND JONATHAN
Test

1. What is the Scripture reference and date for the Deaths of Saul and Jonathan?

   _____

   _____

2. Why wouldn't David kill Saul even though Saul was trying to kill him?

   _____

   _____

   _____

3. Where was David living while it was unsafe for him in Israel?

   _____

   _____

   _____

4. Describe the events surrounding Saul's death.

   _____

   _____

   _____

   _____

   _____

5. Who else died with Saul in the battle?

   _____

   _____

   _____

THE DEATHS OF SAUL AND JONATHAN
Test, Page 2

6. What did the soldier tell David about how Saul died?

_____

_____

_____

7. How did David respond to the soldier?

_____

_____

_____

8. What is "The Song of the Bow?"

_____

_____

_____

Review

1. Why did the Israelites take the Ark into battle?

_____

_____

_____

_____

2. Who was anointed as judges when Samuel grew old?

_____

_____

_____

THE DEATHS OF SAUL AND JONATHAN
Test, Page 3

3. Why did Samuel think that Eliab would be the next king after Saul?

_____

_____

_____

4. From which of the twelve tribes was David?

_____

_____

5. Where was David when Samuel came to anoint him as the next king of Israel?

_____

_____

_____

6. What was the challenge that Goliath made?

_____

_____

_____

_____

_____

THE DEATHS OF SAUL AND JONATHAN
Test, Page 4

7. List all of the titles, Scripture references, and dates studied so far.

_____

_____

_____

_____

_____

_____

_____

_____

_____

_____

_____

_____

_____

_____

_____

_____

DAVIDIC KINGDOM
Worksheet

1. What is the Scripture reference and date for the Davidic Kingdom?

   _____

   _____

2. From what town was David?

   _____

   _____

3. What great military feat gave David favor in the eyes of the army and Saul?

   _____

   _____

   _____

   _____

4. Why did Saul become jealous of David?

   _____

   _____

   _____

   _____

   _____

   _____

Davidic Kingdom
Worksheet, Page 2

5. What did David have to do since Saul was trying to kill him?

   _____

   _____

   _____

6. About how long did David reign?

   _____

   _____

7. David was the _____ and most _____ king of Israel.

DAVIDIC KINGDOM
Project 1—Bible Reading

Have the students read one or more stories about David's rule from the passages suggested below. Then write a paragraph on each story read about what happened. For teachers with multiple students it is suggested that the stories be divided among the students. When each student has completed his assignment, they can take turns reading their paragraphs to the others.

Story Passages

Civil War with Ishbosheth (II Samuel 2)
God's Covenant with David (II Samuel 7)
David's Kindness to Mephibosheth (II Samuel 9)
David takes a Census (II Samuel 24)

_____

_____

_____

_____

_____

_____

_____

_____

_____

_____

_____

_____

_____

DAVIDIC KINGDOM
Project 2

David's (and his son Solomon's) reign over Israel is considered the height of the kingdom. During this time, the kingdom was expanded to cover the most territory. They enjoyed military dominance (and this led to a time of peace during Solomon's reign because no one wanted to challenge them). There was great wealth and development. David established Jerusalem as his capital and Solomon built the temple. And the kingdom prospered under the rule of godly and wise kings. *Draw four pictures below depicting four different strengths of the kingdom during this time.*

DAVIDIC KINGDOM
Test

1. What is the Scripture reference and date for the Davidic Kingdom?

   _____

   _____

2. Who was the father of David?

   _____

   _____

3. What great military feat gave David favor in the eyes of the army and Saul?

   _____

   _____

   _____

4. What happened because the people cheered more for David than for Saul?

   _____

   _____

   _____

5. Why did David have to live as an outlaw?

   _____

   _____

6. After what event could David stop living as an outlaw and return to be the new king of Israel?

   _____

   _____

7. About how long did David reign?

   _____

   _____

8. David is known as the most _____ king of Israel.

DAVIDIC KINGDOM
Review

1. Who was Othniel?

   _____

   _____

   _____

   _____

   _____

2. What did Hannah vow that she
   would do if God blessed her
   with a child?

   _____

   _____

   _____

3. Who was Israel's first king?

   _____

   _____

4. Who was the father of Israel?

   _____

   _____

5. God commanded Saul to kill every _____ and every

   _____ of the Amalekites.

6. Why did Saul want to kill David?

   _____

   _____

   _____

DAVIDIC KINGDOM
Review, Page 2

7. List all of the titles, Scripture references, and dates studied so far.

_____

_____

_____

_____

_____

_____

_____

_____

_____

_____

_____

_____

_____

_____

_____

_____

_____

THE CONQUEST OF JERUSALEM
Worksheet

1. What is the Scripture reference and date for the Conquest of Jerusalem?

   _____

   _____

2. Who was Saul's son who some followed as their king?

   _____

   _____

   _____

3. Name the two men who claimed to be king after Saul died. Which regions supported each man?

   _____

   _____

   _____

4. How did David become the one king of Israel?

   _____

   _____

   _____

   _____

5. Who was living at the stronghold that David wanted?

   _____

   _____

   _____

6. How did David get into the stronghold to take over?

   _____

   _____

   _____

THE CONQUEST OF JERUSALEM
Worksheet, Page 2

7. What was the name of the mountain where David took the stronghold?

_____

_____

_____

8. Name three things given to David by the king of Tyre.

_____

_____

_____

_____

9. Why was God blessing David and establishing him as king?

_____

_____

_____

THE CONQUEST OF JERUSALEM
Project 1—Bible Reading

Read about David's conquest of Jerusalem in II Samuel 5. Choosing from the words in the text, fill in the blanks below with the appropriate parts of speech.

Nouns	Verbs	Adjectives
_____	_____	_____
_____	_____	_____
_____	_____	_____
_____	_____	
_____	_____	

Adverbs	Articles	Prepositional Phrases
_____	_____	_____
_____	_____	_____
		_____
		_____
		_____
		_____

THE CONQUEST OF JERUSALEM
Project 2—Zion

In II Samuel 5:7 Zion is referred to for the first time in the Bible. Originally, "Zion" was the name of a fortified mound. Eventually it came to refer to the whole city of Jerusalem and after that, the entire nation of Israel. Read the following verses and discuss how the concept of "Zion" changed over time.

II Samuel 5:7

Isaiah 2:2–3

Psalm 149:1–4

Hebrews 12:22

Revelation 14:1

CONQUEST OF JERUSALEM
Project 3—Design a City

David chose the stronghold on Mt. Zion for his capital city. Remember the unusual way in which his soldiers were able to enter and capture the stronghold from the Jebusites. After taking the city, David fortified his city. Imagine you were building a city from the beginning rather than improving on an existing city as David did. How would you set up an ideal city? *This project allows students to design and draw their own city with its surrounding area. In this drawing students must include a royal palace, temple, markets, housing, sheepfolds, fields, roads, and water supply. Use the map below or be creative with the landscape as you establish the location of each of the required elements. Be sure to consider a city's need for defense. Also remember that some parts of a city are considered sacred or special. These places would be set apart from the common places. If you wish, you may build in a fatal flaw to your city. Just like the city of Jebus, you may leave a weak spot in your design.*

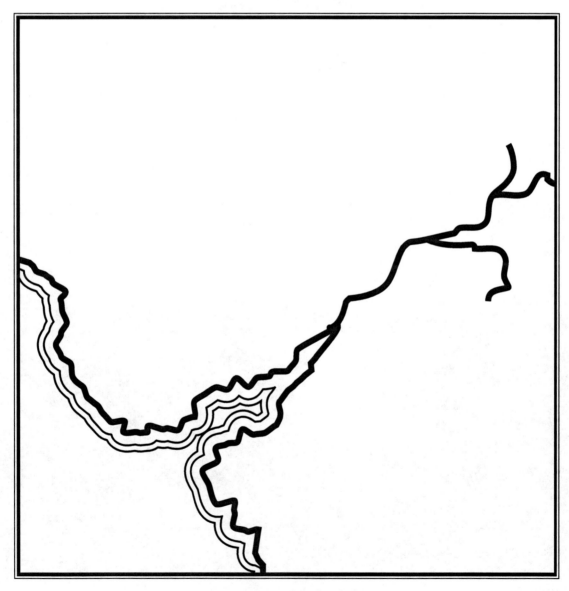

THE CONQUEST OF JERUSALEM
Test

1. What is the Scripture reference and date for the Conquest of Jerusalem?

    _____

    _____

2. Who was Ish-Bosheth?

    _____

    _____

3. Name the two men who claimed to be king after Saul died. Which regions supported each man?

    _____

    _____

    _____

    _____

4. What happened that allowed David to become the one king of Israel?

    _____

    _____

    _____

5. Who were the Jebusites?

    _____

    _____

    _____

THE CONQUEST OF JERUSALEM
Test, Page 2

6. Describe how David got into the stronghold to take over.

_____

_____

_____

_____

_____

7. What was Mount Zion?

_____

_____

_____

8. Who provided David with cedar trees, stone masons, and carpenters? For what were these supplies being used?

_____

_____

_____

9. Why was God blessing David and establishing him as King?

_____

_____

_____

THE CONQUEST OF JERUSALEM
Review, Page 3

1. How did Samson lose his great strength?

_____

_____

2. What happened in the Philistine cities in which Ark was kept?

_____

_____

_____

3. Who was Jesse's youngest son?

_____

4. What did David do to help Saul when he was troubled by the evil spirit?

_____

_____

5. Why couldn't David use Saul's armor?

_____

_____

6. How did Jonathan let David know that Saul was trying to kill him?

_____

_____

_____

THE CONQUEST OF JERUSALEM
Review, Page 4

7. List all of the titles, Scripture references, and dates studied so far.

_____

_____

_____

_____

_____

_____

_____

_____

_____

_____

_____

_____

_____

_____

_____

_____

_____

THE ARK ENTHRONED IN JERUSALEM
Worksheet

1. What is the Scripture reference and date for the Ark Enthroned in Jerusalem?

   _____

   _____

2. How were the Israelites supposed to move the Ark?

   _____

   _____

   _____

   _____

3. How did the Israelites wrongly try to move the Ark? From whom were they copying this method?

   _____

   _____

   _____

   _____

4. What did Uzzah do? What happened to him?

   _____

   _____

   _____

   _____

5. How did God treat the house of Obed-Edom?

   _____

   _____

   _____

THE ARK ENTHRONED IN JERUSALEM
Worksheet, Page 2

6. Describe the sacrifices that David made the second time they moved the Ark.

_____

_____

_____

_____

_____

7. What was David doing as the Ark was brought into Jerusalem?

_____

_____

_____

8. Who did not like David's actions? What was her punishment?

_____

_____

_____

_____

THE ARK ENTHRONED IN JERUSALEM
Project 1–Bible Reading

Read in II Samuel 6 about the Ark being brought to Jerusalem. Then complete the word find below and be sure to know what each word has to do with the story.

```
C A R R T S O B E D E D O M A B
I O X A N A S X B H J K L P O I
N I N S T R U M E N T S R T Y U
S Q W T E N S T E N N T S I I X
T S T U M B L D M I C H A E L S
R U D M B U X O M S R D A V I D
U N E B A Z N N E D A S T E N T
M D S L R Z S D M S I X E M I L
N I P E R A M E I S S V E R I S
T G I D R H M S C G I P R E S S
S N S Q E N A P H S N S S S B C
U I C W N B S I A Q S I S S A A
Z F A E Z V D S L W E R F S R R
Z E R R Z C F E B U S T A I R E
I I T T Y X G D A N C E D S E Y
H D O B E D E D O O M N B V N D
```

cart	Obededom	tent
instruments	six	raisins
stumbled	danced	undignified
Uzzah	Michal	barren
oxen	despised	

THE ARK IS ENTHRONED IN JERUSALEM
Project 2

In the blank write "Righteous" if the statement was something with which God was pleased. Write "Sinful" if the statement explains something that is sinful.

1. _____ The Israelites carried the Ark on poles.

2. _____ Uzzah touched the Ark to steady it.

3. _____ David wanted to bring the Ark to Jerusalem.

4. _____ They sacrificed oxen and sheep every six paces.

5. _____ The Israelites copied off the pagan Philistines.

6. _____ David danced before the Lord.

7. _____ David told Michal that he would humble himself even more.

8. _____ The Israelites transported the Ark on a cart.

9. _____ The Levites carried the Ark.

THE ARK ENTHRONED IN JERUSALEM
Test

1. What is the Scripture reference and date for The Ark Enthroned in Jerusalem?

   _____

   _____

2. How were the Israelites supposed to move the Ark?

   _____

   _____

   _____

3. How did the Israelites wrongly try to move the Ark? From whom did they copy this?

   _____

   _____

   _____

   _____

   _____

4. Who reached up to steady the Ark? What happened to him?

   _____

   _____

   _____

   _____

   _____

5. How often did they make a sacrifice the second time they moved the Ark.

   _____

   _____

   _____

   _____

THE ARK ENTHRONED IN JERUSALEM
Test, Page 2

6. Who danced before the Lord as the Ark was brought into Jerusalem?

_____

_____

_____

7. Who was Michal?

_____

_____

_____

_____

8. What was Michal's sin?

_____

_____

_____

_____

Review

1. Write a paragraph about your favorite judge.

_____

_____

_____

_____

_____

_____

_____

THE ARK ENTHRONED IN JERUSALEM
Test, Page 3

2. List all of the titles, Scripture references, and dates studied so far.

_____

_____

_____

_____

_____

_____

_____

_____

_____

_____

_____

_____

_____

_____

_____

_____

_____

_____

_____

_____

DAVID WRITES MANY PSALMS
Worksheet

1. Who wrote many of the Psalms?

   _____

   _____

2. Name the five types of psalms.

   _____

   _____

   _____

3. Describe psalms of lament.

   _____

   _____

   _____

   _____

DAVID WRITES MANY PSALMS
Worksheet, Page 2

4. What is an example of a psalm of confession?

_____

_____

_____

_____

_____

5. Describe imprecatory psalms.

_____

_____

_____

_____

_____

6. What is the approximate date of the psalms?

_____

_____

DAVID WRITES MANY PSALMS
Project 1—Bible Reading

Read Psalms 129, 88, 33, 38, and 9:1-6. Write in the blanks which type of psalm each is. Then answer each question according to the Psalm.

PRAISE_____

What about God is worthy of praise?

_____

_____

THANKSGIVING_____

What has God done for the author?

_____

_____

LAMENT_____

How is the author asking God to help him?

_____

_____

IMPRECATORY_____

Like what does the author ask God to make his enemies?

_____

_____

CONFESSION_____

Name three ways in which sin was affecting the author.

_____

_____

_____

DAVID WRITES MANY PSALMS
Project 2—Bible Reading

Read Psalm 37. This psalm of David discusses the Heritage of the Righteous and the Calamity of the Wicked, or what will happen to both the righteous and the wicked. In the chart below, write phrases or sentences from the psalm that describe what the righteous and the wicked will receive.

The Heritage of the Righteous	*The Calamity of the Wicked*
_____	_____
_____	_____
_____	_____
_____	_____
_____	_____
_____	_____
_____	_____
_____	_____
_____	_____
_____	_____
_____	_____
_____	_____
_____	_____

DAVID WRITES MANY PSALMS
Project 3—Parallelism in the Psalms

The main poetic technique used in the psalms is called parallelism. There are many forms of parallelism, but here is a simple explanation. The psalmist writes one line (or set of lines) and then in the next line (or set of lines), he restates what was said in other words. This may sound like repetition, but if you look closely at the second line, you frequently see that the psalmist has expanded or explained his previous line.

Read Psalm 107 and look inside each verse for parts one and two of the parallelism. Then have students try to identify how the psalmist has expanded on the first part of each parallelism. Here is some guidance for the first three verses.

VERSE 1   Part 1   Oh give thanks to the Lord, for He is good!

           Part 2   For His mercy endures forever.

           Part 2   answers how the Lord is good.

VERSE 2   Part 1   Let the redeemed of the Lord say so,

           Part 2   Whom He has redeemed from the hand of the enemy,

           Part 2   answers from whom they were redeemed.

VERSE 3   Part 1   And gathered out of the lands,

           Part 2   From the east and the west, from the north and the south.

           Part 2   answers from where they were gathered.

In some verses it is harder to explain how the second part of the parallelism expands upon the first part. Merely identifying the two parts is sufficient.

David Writes Many Psalms
Project 3, Page 2

Students can now write a second part to each parallelism that is begun below. Remember, the length of each part is not important, nor is rhyming.

Do not hide your face from me,

_____

_____

The nations shall fear the name of the Lord,

_____

_____

As for man, his days are like grass,

_____

_____

The Lord laid the foundations of the earth,

_____

_____

For the Lord will not cast off his people,

_____

_____

DAVID WRITES MANY PSALMS
Test

1. Name the five types of psalms.

    _____

    _____

    _____

    _____

2. In what type of psalm does the author cry out to God for help?

    _____

    _____

    _____

3. Psalm 51 is an example of what type of psalm?

    _____

    _____

    _____

4. What is Psalm 51 about?

    _____

    _____

    _____

5. In what type of psalm does the author pray for God to judge his enemies?

    _____

    _____

    _____

6. What is the date for David Writes Many Psalms.

    _____

    _____

DAVID WRITES MANY PSALMS
Test, Page 2

Review

1. On the night that Samuel was called by God, what did God tell Samuel would happen to Eli's family?

_____

_____

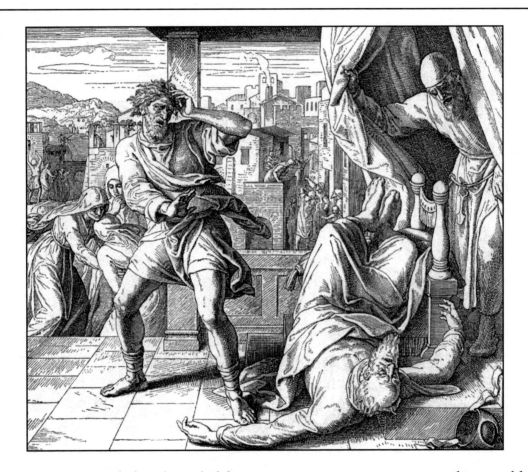

2. The Israelites demanded to be ruled by _____ so they could be like _____.

DAVID WRITES MANY PSALMS
Test, Page 3

3. What fighting experience did David relate to Saul when he told Saul he would fight Goliath?

_____

_____

_____

_____

4. What was the lie that the soldier told David about how Saul died?

_____

_____

_____

5. About how long did David reign?

_____

_____

6. How did the Israelites wrongly try to move the Ark?

_____

_____

_____

7. List all of the titles, Scripture references, and dates studied so far.

_____

_____

_____

_____

_____

_____

_____

7. (continued)

_____

_____

_____

_____

_____

_____

_____

_____

_____

_____

_____

_____

_____

DAVID AND BATHSHEBA
Worksheet

1. What is the Scripture reference and date for David and Bathsheba?

   _____

   _____

2. What was the sin of David and Bathsheba?

   _____

   _____

   _____

3. Who was Bathsheba's husband?

   _____

   _____

4. How did David first try to hide his sin? Why did that attempt not work?

   _____

   _____

   _____

   _____

5. What did David have Joab do?

   _____

   _____

   _____

   _____

6. Who then married Bathsheba?

   _____

   _____

   _____

DAVID AND BATHSHEBA
Worksheet, Page 2

7. Who was Nathan?

_____

_____

_____

8. What happened to the
child born from the
sinful union of David
and Bathsheba?

_____

_____

_____

_____

_____

_____

_____

9. Who was another son born to David and Bathsheba?

_____

_____

_____

DAVID AND BATHSHEBA
Project 1—Bible Reading

Read about the story of David and Bathsheba in II Samuel 11–12. Then answer the following questions.

1. What should David have been doing instead of staying home in Jerusalem?

   _____

   _____

2. Why did Uriah sleep at the door of the king's house when he was called home from the war?

   _____

   _____

3. David tried a second night to get Uriah to go home. What did David do to Uriah so that he might go home?

   _____

   _____

4. Joab put Uriah on the _____ and he was _____.

5. Describe the parable that Nathan told David to show him his sin.

   _____

   _____

   _____

   _____

   _____

DAVID AND BATHSHEBA
Project 2—Psalm 51

Psalm 51 is David's confession of his sin with Bathsheba. Read the psalm and answer the following questions.

1. Write two sins which you know David is talking about in verses 1-3 even though he does not state them.

   _____

   _____

   _____

2. What does David say about the "innermost being" in verse 6?

   _____

   _____

   _____

3. What does David say that he will be like if God washes him (verse 7)?

   _____

   _____

   _____

4. What does David ask for in verse 10?

   _____

   _____

   _____

DAVID AND BATHSHEBA
Project 2—Psalm 51, Page 2

5. If God gives David his requests in verses 10–12, what will David then do?

    _____

    _____

    _____

6. What are the sacrifices of God named in verse 17?

    _____

    _____

    _____

DAVID AND BATHSHEBA
Project 3—Symbolism in Church Art

The picture on the flashcard depicts David seeing Bathsheba take a bath. Yet that is not all that is in the picture. To decode or "read" this illustration it is helpful to know that long ago, when people were creating art for the church, they used colors and animals and shapes to tell stories in pictures for those who could not read. Everyone knew what the symbols represented, just like in our time, everyone knows when they see a swoosh it means sneakers, a golden "M" means hamburgers and a talking tiger wearing a big red bib means sugar-coated corn flakes.

Find the following elements in the picture then color in the illustration or create your own picture using some of the ancient church art symbols below.

Colors: Gold is a symbol of pure light, the heavenly realm where God lives. Even though David thinks he is committing a sin in secret, the light of God is all around him. Purple represents royalty and the color white is a symbol for purity and innocence.

Cross: The cross is a symbol for Christ and when it is in a halo, it shows the viewer that the bearer of that halo is a member of the Trinity.

Dove: Almost every time one sees a dove in church art it is a representation of the Holy Spirit.

Fox: Often symbolizing the Devil, the fox represents cunning and guile. Sin is crouching on David's side of the picture.

Lamb: The lamb is a symbol for Jesus, especially when it has a triangular halo. The lamb in this picture is more closely linked with the story Nathan told to David and is the intended prey of the fox.

Nudity: A nude body often was a symbol for purity and innocence.

Three: The number three represents God as he exists in the Trinity (Father, Son and Holy Spirit). What do you see three of in the picture? Hint: In the book of Romans, it is said that we can see things about God even in nature.

Water: Water is usually a symbol of purifying and cleansing due to it's use in the sacrament of Baptism. Sometimes it can symbolize trouble as in Psalm 69:1–2. Here it is being used in this latter way.

DAVID AND BATHSHEBA
Test

1. What is the Scripture reference and date for David and Bathsheba?

   _____

   _____

2. What was the sin of David and Bathsheba?

   _____

   _____

   _____

   _____

3. Who was Uriah?

   _____

   _____

4. How did Uriah die? Why was he killed?

   _____

   _____

   _____

5. Who were the two people that secretly arranged for Uriah's death?

   _____

   _____

6. Who married Bathsheba after Uriah died?

   _____

   _____

   _____

   _____

DAVID AND BATHSHEBA
Test, Page 2

7. Who was God's prophet that rebuked David for his sin?

_____

_____

8. What was one punishment for David's sin?

_____

_____

_____

9. Who was another son of David and Bathsheba?

_____

_____

_____

Review

1. What did Saul do for King Agag that caused God to reject him as king?

_____

_____

_____

2. Describe Goliath.

_____

_____

_____

DAVID AND BATHSHEBA
Test, Page 3

3. How was Jonathan related to Saul?

_____

_____

_____

4. Where was David living while it was unsafe for him in Israel?

_____

_____

_____

5. How did Saul die?

_____

_____

_____

6. What happened because the people cheered more for David than for Saul?

_____

_____

_____

7. List all of the titles, Scripture references, and dates studied so far.

_____

_____

_____

_____

_____

_____

7. (continued)

_____

_____

_____

_____

_____

_____

_____

_____

_____

_____

_____

_____

_____

DAVID AND ABSALOM
Worksheet

1. What is the Scripture reference and date for David and Absalom?

   _____

   _____

2. Describe Absalom. How was he related to David?

   _____

   _____

   _____

   _____

3. How did Absalom steal the hearts of the men of Israel?

   _____

   _____

   _____

4. When Absalom had himself crowned king, what did David do?

   _____

   _____

   _____

5. Who was the follower of David who was sent to give Absalom bad advice?

   _____

   _____

   _____

6. What should Absalom have done when he had David on the run?

   _____

   _____

   _____

DAVID AND ABSALOM
Worksheet, Page 2

7. What did Absalom do?

_____

_____

_____

_____

8. How did Absalom become stuck in the tree?

_____

_____

_____

9. How did Absalom die? Who killed him?

_____

_____

_____

_____

10. How did David react to the death of Absalom?

_____

_____

_____

DAVID AND ABSALOM
Project 1—Bible Reading

Read about David and Absalom in II Samuel 15, 18. Then draw three scenes as described by the captions below them. Use conversation bubbles to include the important words that were said.

Absalom steals the hearts of the people

David flees Jerusalem

Absalom's death

DAVID AND ABSALOM
Project 2

David wrote Psalm 3 when his son Absalom crowned himself king. David had lost the loyalty of most of the kingdom and had to flee from Jerusalem. Read Psalm 3. Then draw a picture below of how Absalom was killed.

DAVID AND ABSALOM
Test

1. What is the Scripture reference and date for David and Absalom?

    _____

    _____

2. Describe Absalom. How was he related to David?

    _____

    _____

    _____

3. How did Absalom steal the hearts of the men of Israel?

    _____

    _____

    _____

4. What did David do when Absalom had himself crowned king?

    _____

    _____

    _____

5. Who was Hushai?

    _____

    _____

    _____

6. What should Absalom have done when he had David on the run?

    _____

    _____

    _____

DAVID AND ABSALOM
Test, Page 2

7. What was Hushai's bad advice?

_____

_____

_____

8. Before the battle, how did David tell his soldiers to deal with Absalom?

_____

_____

_____

9. Describe the death of Absalom.

_____

_____

_____

_____

_____

10. How did David react to the death of Absalom?

_____

_____

_____

Review

1. What unusual weapon did Samson use to kill a thousand Philistines?

_____

_____

DAVID AND ABSALOM
Test, Page 3

2. What happened when the Ark was kept in Dagon's temple?

_____

_____

_____

3. How many days did Goliath come forward to make his challenge?

_____

_____

4. What is the "Song of the Bow"?

_____

_____

_____

5. Describe how David got into the stronghold of Jebus to take over.

_____

_____

_____

6. What happened to Uzzah?

_____

_____

7. List all of the titles, Scripture references, and dates studied so far.

_____

_____

_____

_____

_____

_____

7. (continued)

_____

_____

_____

_____

_____

_____

_____

_____

_____

_____

_____

_____

_____

_____

_____

_____

Solomon's Reign
Worksheet

1. What is the Scripture reference and date for Solomon's Reign?

   _____

   _____

2. Who was Solomon's father?

   _____

   _____

3. What did Solomon request of God?

   _____

   _____

   _____

4. During Solomon's reign there was

   _____ in Israel.

5. Describe the temple.

   _____

   _____

   _____

   _____

   _____

   _____

   _____

   _____

SOLOMON'S REIGN
Worksheet, Page 2

6. Who came to visit Solomon to see the temple and his wealth?

_____

_____

_____

7. Late in life Solomon was tempted by _____,

    and he turned from _____.

8. How long did Solomon reign?

_____

_____

_____

SOLOMON'S REIGN
Project 1—Bible Reading

Read in I Kings 1 about Solomon's brother's attempt to take the throne instead of Solomon.
Then write a paragraph about what happened.

_____

_____

_____

_____

_____

_____

_____

_____

_____

_____

_____

_____

_____

_____

_____

_____

SOLOMON'S REIGN
Project 2—Proverbs

Many of the proverbs teach lessons about the character of a godly person and a foolish person. Fill the blanks with a word or phrase that describes the character of a godly person.

Prov. 25:16 _____

Prov. 25:17 _____

Prov. 27:18 _____

Prov. 28:27 _____

Prov. 29:11 _____

Prov. 29:20 _____

Prov. 29:23 _____

Many of the proverbs are addressed to a son. While most of the advice to the son can be applied to women, Proverbs 31 gives a separate description of a woman of excellence. Write the characteristics described in the following verses found in Proverbs 31.

v. 15 _____

v. 16 _____

v. 20 _____

v. 21 _____

v. 25 _____

_____

_____

v. 26 _____

v. 31 _____

SOLOMON'S REIGN
Test

1. What is the Scripture reference and date for Solomon's Reign?

   _____

   _____

2. What did Solomon request of God?

   _____

   _____

   _____

3. What else did God give Solomon because he was pleased with his request?

   _____

   _____

4. Solomon built _____. Describe it.

   _____

   _____

   _____

   _____

5. Why did the Queen of Sheba and other nobles come to visit Solomon?

   _____

   _____

6. What happened to Solomon later in life?

   _____

   _____

   _____

SOLOMON'S REIGN
Test, Page 2

7. How long did Solomon reign?

_____

_____

8. Who became king after Solomon?

_____

_____

_____

Review

1. Name three judges.

_____

_____

_____

2. What was David taking to his brothers when he found out about Goliath's challenge?

_____

_____

_____

3. Why wouldn't David kill Saul even though Saul was trying to kill him?

_____

_____

_____

SOLOMON'S REIGN
Test, Page 3

4. Who provided David with cedar trees, stone masons, and carpenters for his city?

_____

_____

_____

_____

5. Who danced before the Lord as the Ark was brought into Jerusalem?

_____

_____

_____

6. List all of the titles, Scripture references, and dates studied so far.

_____

_____

_____

_____

_____

_____

_____

_____

_____

_____

_____

_____

_____

_____

6. (continued)

_____

_____

_____

_____

_____

_____

_____

_____

_____

SOLOMON GIVEN WISDOM
Worksheet

1. What is the Scripture reference and date for Solomon Given Wisdom?

   _____

   _____

2. What characteristic did Solomon display when God appeared to him?

   _____

   _____

   _____

   _____

   _____

3. When did God appear to Solomon? What did God ask Solomon?

   _____

   _____

   _____

   _____

   _____

4. What did Solomon request? Why?

   _____

   _____

   _____

   _____

   _____

Solomon Given Wisdom
Worksheet, Page 2

5. What two things did God also give to Solomon along with his request?

_____

_____

_____

_____

6. Why did nobles from far away lands come to visit Solomon?

_____

_____

_____

_____

_____

SOLOMON GIVEN WISDOM
Project 1—Bible Reading

Read in I Kings 3 about Solomon's request for wisdom. Then fill in the spaces below with the details of the case that was brought before Solomon.

The parties involved:

_____

_____

_____

The problem:

_____

_____

_____

_____

Solomon's solution:

_____

_____

_____

How the parties reacted to Solomon's solution:

_____

_____

_____

Solomon's final verdict:

_____

_____

_____

_____

SOLOMON GIVEN WISDOM
Project 2

Read Proverbs 3:1-12. In the verses listed in the left column, look for a word that fits the box outline next to it.

Verse—

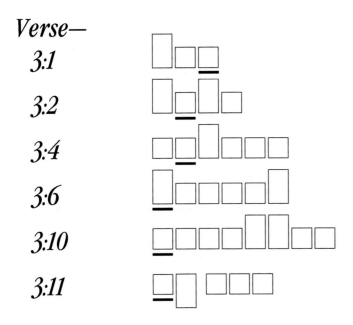

3:1

3:2

3:4

3:6

3:10

3:11

Now write below the letters that you placed in the underlined boxes. What word do these

letters spell? _ _ _ _ _ _

SOLOMON GIVEN WISDOM
Test

1. What is the Scripture reference and date for Solomon Given Wisdom?

   _____

   _____

2. Describe the circumstances in which Solomon was given wisdom?

   _____

   _____

   _____

   _____

   _____

   _____

3. Why did Solomon ask for wisdom?

   _____

   _____

   _____

   _____

4. What two things did God give to Solomon along with wisdom?

   _____

   _____

   _____

   _____

5. Who came from far away lands to witness Solomon's wisdom?

   _____

   _____

SOLOMON GIVEN WISDOM
Test, Page 2

Review

1. What happened to the man who told David that he had killed King Saul?

   _____

   _____

2. David is known as the most _____ king of Israel.

3. After Saul died, who other than David claimed to be king of Israel?

   _____

   _____

4. How often did David and the Israelites make a sacrifice the second time
   they moved the Ark.

   _____

   _____

   _____

5. In what type of psalm does the author cry out to God for help?

   _____

   _____

6. List all of the titles, Scripture references, and dates studied so far.

   _____

   _____

   _____

   _____

   _____

   _____

   _____

6. (continued)

_____

_____

_____

_____

_____

_____

_____

_____

_____

_____

_____

_____

_____

_____

THE WRITINGS OF SOLOMON
Worksheet

1. What is the Scripture reference and date for the Writings of Solomon?

   _____

   _____

2. Name two words that describe what things were like during Solomon's reign.

   _____

   _____

   _____

   _____

3. Even more than his father, _____, Solomon was a patron of the _____.

4. About how many proverbs did Solomon write?

   _____

   _____

5. What is one of the oldest philosophy books in the world?

   _____

   _____

6. According to Ecclesiastes, what is meaningless?

   _____

   _____

7. What is man's greatest goal in life according to Ecclesiastes?

   _____

   _____

   _____

THE WRITINGS OF SOLOMON
Project 1—Bible Reading

Many of the proverbs use a picture or comparison to teach a lesson. Choose four proverbs to illustrate in the boxes below. Write words to label what is being compared to the picture or write a brief explanation of the proverb under the picture. Also write the reference with your pictures.

PROV. 11:22   PROV. 25:20   PROV. 25:24   PROV. 25:28   PROV. 27:22   PROV. 28:3

THE WRITINGS OF SOLOMON
Project 2—Proverbs 10

A main focus of the Proverbs is to contrast the righteous (wise person) and the wicked (fool). Read Proverbs 10. For each verse on the chart write how the righteous and the wicked are described.

	Righteous	*Wicked*
v. 1		
v. 4		
v. 5		
v. 16		
v. 20		
v. 23		
v. 25		
v. 27		

THE WRITINGS OF SOLOMON
Project 3—Ecclesiastes

Read Ecclesiastes 1:1–12.
DEFINITION: futile: *meaningless* or *without value.*

1. What does Solomon call himself in Ecclesiastes 1:1?

   _____

   _____

2. In verse 2, Solomon says, "All is _____."

3. List two things in nature that Solomon says move in circles and therefore never get
   anywhere. (verses 4–7)

   _____

   _____

   _____

   _____

4. Verse 9 states that there is nothing new _____ _____ _____.

5. In Ecclesiastes 1:12–18 Solomon considers _____ and determines
   that it is _____.

6. In Ecclesiastes 2:1–11 Solomon considers _____ and determines
   that it is _____.

7. Solomon again considers _____ in Ecclesiastes 2:12–17.
   What reason does he give that wisdom is vanity in Eccl. 2:16?

   _____

   _____

   _____

8. In Ecclesiastes 2:18–23 Solomon considers _____ and determines
   that it is _____.

THE WRITINGS OF SOLOMON
Project 3—Ecclesiastes, Page 2

9. In Ecclesiastes 2:24-26 Solomon considers _____ and determines

   that it is _____.

10. Read Ecclesiastes 3:1-8. List four things for which Solomon says there is a time.

_____

_____

_____

_____

11. Ecclesiastes 12:13-14 is the conclusion of Solomon's book.

    What does Solomon say we should do with our lives?

_____

_____

    Why? (verse 14)

_____

_____

WRITINGS OF SOLOMON
Test

1. What is the Scripture reference and date for Writings of Solomon?

   _____

   _____

2. Solomon's reign was marked by _____ and _____
   which come from wise rule.

3. Of what was Solomon a patron?

   _____

   _____

   _____

4. About how many proverbs did Solomon write?

   _____

   _____

   _____

5. Ecclesiastes is one of the earliest _____ books in the world.

6. According to Ecclesiastes, what is meaningless?

   _____

   _____

   _____

7. What is man's greatest goal in life according to Ecclesiastes?

   _____

   _____

   _____

WRITINGS OF SOLOMON
Test, Page 2

Review

1. By calling to the boy that the _____ were beyond him, Jonathan warned David that he should flee for his life.

2. What was Mt. Zion?

   _____

   _____

   _____

3. Who was Uriah?

   _____

   _____

4. What happened to Solomon later in life?

   _____

   _____

   _____

5. What two things did God give to Solomon along with wisdom?

   _____

   _____

   _____

6. List all of the titles, Scripture references, and dates studied so far.

   _____

   _____

   _____

   _____

   _____

   _____

6. (continued)

_____

_____

_____

_____

_____

_____

_____

_____

_____

_____

_____

_____

_____

_____

_____

_____

_____

_____

_____

THE TEMPLE IS BUILT
Worksheet

1. What is the Scripture reference and date for the Temple is Built?

   _____

   _____

2. From what country did Solomon obtain cedar trees?

   _____

   _____

3. Name two things that Hiram, king of Tyre provided for Solomon.

   _____

   _____

   _____

4. What did the metal worker do?

   _____

   _____

5. Describe where the blocks for the temple were cut and fitted.

   _____

   _____

   _____

   _____

6. Describe the interior of the temple.

   _____

   _____

   _____

   _____

   _____

THE TEMPLE IS BUILT
Worksheet, Page 2

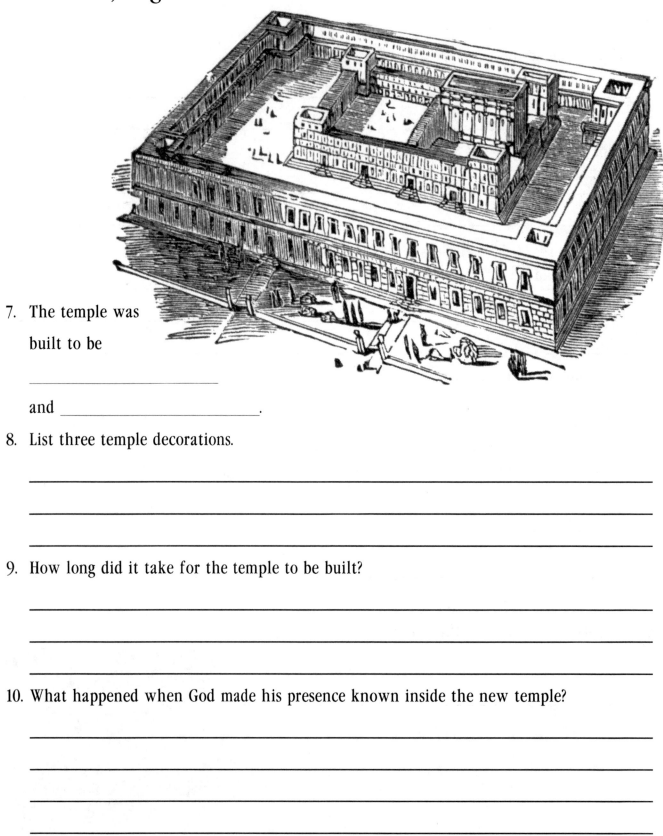

7. The temple was
   built to be

   _____

   and _____.

8. List three temple decorations.

   _____

   _____

   _____

9. How long did it take for the temple to be built?

   _____

   _____

   _____

10. What happened when God made his presence known inside the new temple?

   _____

   _____

   _____

   _____

THE TEMPLE IS BUILT
Project 1—Bible Reading

As you read in I Kings 6-8 about the building of the temple, make a list of building supplies (woods and metals) and decorations used in this magnificent architectural structure.

Building Supplies

_____

_____

_____

_____

_____

_____

_____

Decorations

_____

_____

_____

_____

_____

_____

_____

THE TEMPLE IS BUILT
Project 2—Art for Worship

Church buildings come in all shapes and sizes—some more ornate than a wedding cake and others as plain as a cracker. Yet when God was designing (I Chron. 28:12) a building for worshipping Him, a very important element was the building's appearance. Francis Schaeffer in the book Art and the Bible discusses the importance of the visual arts in God's design for the temple when he writes:

> What, therefore, was to be in the temple? For one thing, the temple was filled with artwork. "And he [Solomon] garnished [covered] the house with precious stones for beauty" (2 Chron. 3:6). Notice this carefully: The temple was covered with precious stones for beauty. There was no pragmatic reason for the precious stones. They had no utilitarian purpose. God simply wanted beauty in the temple. God is interested in beauty.

Read the verses listed below and in the blanks write what elements were incorporated into the building of the temple not out of architectural necessity but for the sake of being beautiful. If there is time, design a repeating pattern (like wallpaper) based on I Kings 6:29 in the box at the bottom of the page.

I Kings 6:18

_____

I Kings 6:21

_____

I Kings 6:29

_____

I Kings 7:15–18, 22

_____

_____

```


```

THE TEMPLE IS BUILT
Project 3—Soap Masons

The temple that Solomon built was a great architectural feat. All of the cutting was done at the quarry. Imagine how hard it would be to build something without being able to make small adjustments as you pieced things together. This project helps students discover how difficult the task of building the temple was. You may chose to do this as a whole class or in smaller groups if you have a large number of students.

Give each building group or individual a copy of the wall outline below. They will also need a steak knife, cutting surface, ruler, and 5-10 bars of soap.

Students must cut each bar of soap into at least four blocks. Remind students to be careful with the knife. Students must build 2–4 walls (depending on how much soap you were able to provide) as high as they can. Students may measure and plan ahead, but they may not move blocks once they have been cut for a specific location. No cutting adjustments may be made once a cut block is brought to the "building site". Remember, this is to show how difficult the temple building was. Students should not expect great success. Rather, they should feel awe and appreciation.

DOOR

THE TEMPLE IS BUILT
Test

1. What is the Scripture reference and date for the Temple is Built?

   _____

   _____

2. Descibe the story of how the temple was built.

   _____

   _____

   _____

   _____

   _____

   _____

   _____

   _____

   _____

   _____

   _____

   _____

   _____

   _____

   _____

   _____

   _____

   _____

THE TEMPLE IS BUILT
Test, Page 2

Review

1. Who was the priest who raised and taught Samuel?

_____

_____

_____

2. In what type of psalm does the author pray for God to judge his enemies?

_____

_____

3. What was the stronghold that David captured so that he could build a city?

_____

_____

_____

4. What was one punishment for David's sin with Bathsheba?

_____

_____

_____

5. Describe Absalom.

_____

_____

_____

_____

6. How long did Solomon reign?

_____

_____

7. List all of the titles, Scripture references, and dates studied so far.

_____

_____

_____

_____

_____

_____

_____

_____

_____

_____

_____

_____

POMEGRANATES.

THE TEMPLE IS BUILT
Test, Page 3

7.   (continued)

_____

_____

_____

_____

_____

_____

_____

_____

_____

_____

_____

_____

_____

THE QUEEN OF SHEBA VISITS SOLOMON
Worksheet

1. What is the Scripture reference and date for the Queen of Sheba Visits Solomon?

   _____

   _____

2. Why did the Queen of Sheba visit Solomon?

   _____

   _____

   _____

3. Describe the Queen of Sheba's traveling companions.

   _____

   _____

   _____

   _____

   _____

THE QUEEN OF SHEBA VISITS SOLOMON
Worksheet, Page 2

4. How did the queen's time with Solomon go?

_____

_____

_____

_____

5. Who did the Queen of Sheba say was blessed because of Solomon's wisdom?

_____

_____

_____

_____

6. What did the Queen of Sheba give to Solomon?

_____

_____

_____

_____

THE QUEEN OF SHEBA VISITS SOLOMON
Project 1—Bible Reading

Read in I Kings 10:1-13 about the Queen of Sheba's visit with Solomon. Then fill in the text and crossword puzzle below.

The Queen of _____ had heard of Solomon's _____. She
                  (1 across)   (2 across)

came to_____ his wisdom. She brought many _____
             (3 down)   (4 across)

loaded with_____, gold, and precious stones. The queen _____
             (5 down)   (6 across)

Solomon about many things. She found that his _____ and _____ exceeded
                                      (7 down)   (8 across)

what she had heard. Both the queen and Solomon gave each other many _____.
                                                       (9 down)

THE QUEEN OF SHEBA VISITS SOLOMON
Project 2

Use the code to translate each characteristic of the Queen of Sheba.
Then write an explanation of how she displayed that characteristic in the verse listed.

1	2	3	4	5	6	7	8	9	10	11	12	13
A	B	C	D	E	F	G	H	I	J	K	L	M

14	15	16	17	18	19	20	21	22	23	24	25	26
N	O	P	Q	R	S	T	U	V	W	X	Y	Z

1. _____
   16 15 23 5 18 6 21 12

   I Kings 10:1

   _____

2. _____
   19 11 5 16 20 9 3 1 12

   I Kings 10:1

   _____

3. _____
   9 13 16 18 5 19 19 5 4

   I Kings 10:4, 5

   _____

4. _____
   7 15 4 - 6 5 1 18 9 14 7

   I Kings 10:9

   _____

5. _____
   7 5 14 5 18 15 21 19

   I Kings 10:10

   _____

THE QUEEN OF SHEBA VISITS SOLOMON
Test

1. What is the Scripture reference and date for the Queen of Sheba Visits Solomon?

   _____

   _____

2. Solomon was known around the world as a _____ king.

3. Why did the Queen of Sheba visit Solomon?

   _____

   _____

   _____

4. Describe the Queen of Sheba's traveling entourage.

   _____

   _____

   _____

   _____

   _____

5. How did the queen's time with Solomon go?

   _____

   _____

   _____

6. Who did the Queen of Sheba say was blessed because of Solomon's wisdom?

   _____

   _____

   _____

   _____

   _____

7. What did the Queen of Sheba give to Solomon?

_____

_____

_____

_____

_____

_____

Review

1. Describe how Samson's death resulted in the death of many Philistines.

_____

_____

_____

_____

_____

2. Name three types of psalms.

_____

_____

_____

_____

3. What was the sin of David and Bathsheba?

_____

_____

_____

4. Describe the death of Absalom.

_____

_____

_____

_____

_____

5. What did Solomon request of God?

_____

_____

6. List all of the titles, Scripture references, and dates studied so far.

_____

_____

_____

_____

_____

_____

_____

_____

_____

_____

6. (continued)

_____

_____

_____

_____

_____

_____

_____

_____

_____

_____

_____

_____

_____

_____

THE END OF SOLOMON'S REIGN
Worksheet

1. What is the Scripture reference and date for the end of Solomon's reign?

   _____

   _____

2. What did Solomon do late in life?

   _____

   _____

   _____

   _____

3. Why did God command the Israelites not to make covenants with foreigners?

   _____

   _____

   _____

   _____

   _____

THE END OF SOLOMON'S REIGN
Worksheet, Page 2

4. What did Solomon build for his wives?

_____

_____

_____

5. Whom did God raise up against Solomon?

_____

_____

_____

6. What was the greatest punishment Solomon received for his sin?

_____

_____

_____

THE END OF SOLOMON'S REIGN
Project 1—Bible Reading

Read in I Kings 11:1-13 about the end of Solomon's reign. The silly phrases below rhyme with phrases from the story. Write the phrase from the story next to each silly phrase. Then write a sentence using each phrase as it is used in the story. The longer phrases contain small words which are not rhymed. These small words are underlined so that you will know they are not to be changed.

Lauren hives _____ _____

_____

_____

bye faces _____ _____

_____

_____

turned intense _____ _____

_____

_____

learned his part _____ _____

_____

_____

bear the wisdom today _____ _____ _____

_____

not delay the cord _____ _____ _____

_____

THE END OF SOLOMON'S REIGN
Project 2

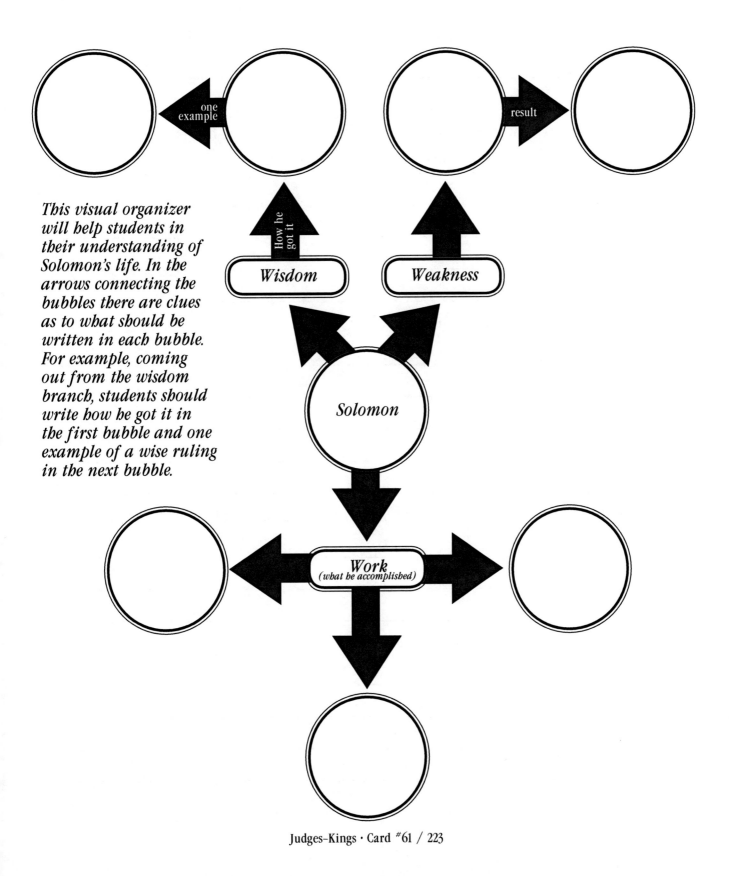

This visual organizer will help students in their understanding of Solomon's life. In the arrows connecting the bubbles there are clues as to what should be written in each bubble. For example, coming out from the wisdom branch, students should write how he got it in the first bubble and one example of a wise ruling in the next bubble.

one example

result

How he got it

Wisdom

Weakness

Solomon

Work
(what he accomplished)

THE END OF SOLOMON'S REIGN
Test

1. What is the Scripture reference and date for the End of Solomon's Reign?

   _____

   _____

2. Describe Solomon's obedience to the law of the Lord late in his life.

   _____

   _____

   _____

   _____

3. Name two sins committed by Solomon late in life?

   _____

   _____

   _____

   _____

4. What did God say would happen if the Israelites made covenants with foreigners?

   _____

   _____

   _____

5. Name two ways in which God punished Solomon for his sin.

   _____

   _____

   _____

   _____

THE END OF SOLOMON'S REIGN
Test, Page 2

Review

1. Who was Michal?

_____

_____

2. Who was God's prophet that rebuked David for his sin?

_____

_____

3. Describe the circumstances in which Solomon was given wisdom?

_____

_____

_____

4. About how many proverbs did Solomon write?

_____

_____

5. What did the Queen of Sheba give to Solomon?

_____

_____

6. List all of the titles, Scripture references, and dates studied so far.

_____

_____

_____

_____

_____

THE END OF SOLOMON'S REIGN
Test, Page 3

6. (continued)

_____

_____

_____

_____

_____

_____

_____

_____

_____

_____

_____

_____

_____

_____

_____

_____

_____

_____

_____

_____

_____

_____

_____

ISRAEL DIVIDES INTO TWO KINGDOMS
Worksheet

1. What is the Scripture reference and date for Israel Divides into Two Kingdoms?

   _____

   _____

2. What did Solomon do that angered God?

   _____

   _____

   _____

3. What was the consequence of Solomon's sin?

   _____

   _____

   _____

4. Why wouldn't the punishment come during Solomon's life?

   _____

   _____

   _____

5. Who was Ahijah? What did he do?

   _____

   _____

   _____

   _____

ISRAEL DIVIDES INTO TWO KINGDOMS
Worksheet, Page 2

6. Why did the tribes rebel against Rehoboam?

_____

_____

_____

_____

7. Who ruled over the ten tribes?

_____

_____

ISRAEL DIVIDES INTO TWO KINGDOMS
Project 1—Bible Reading

Read the account of the division of Israel in I Kings. Especially take note of how Rehoboam handled his first challenge of being king: the people's request for him to lighten the burden of their work. Then fill in the quotes using your own words to summarize the conversation between Rehoboam, the people, and his advisors.

The people said,

"_____

_____"

Rehoboam said,

"_____

_____"

The older advisors said,

"_____

_____"

Rehoboam said,

"_____

_____"

The younger advisors said,

"_____

_____"

Rehoboam told the people,

"_____

_____"

The people told Rehoboam,

"_____

_____"

ISRAEL DIVIDES INTO TWO KINGDOMS
Project 2

    Read I Kings 12:25-33 and then discuss the changes (and the reasons for the changes) made by Jeroboam using the questions below. On the next page, color the Northern and Southern Kingdoms different colors. Cut out the labels and symbols on the right.

    Using an atlas or map locate and label your map with the cities for which you have labels. Glue the pictures of the golden calves next to the cities in which they were built. Put the symbols for capitols next to the city labels for the Northern & Southern capitols. Draw arrows to the North and South and glue the labels that go with each kingdom. Draw arrows and glue the labels for the kings that ruled. Then put the crown symbol next to the kings' names.

1. How did Jeroboam establish new places of worship for the North?

    _____

    _____

    _____

2. Why did Jeroboam do this?

    _____

    _____

    _____

3. Why do you think Jeroboam chose the location of those two cities for new worship sites?

    _____

    _____

    _____

4. List three other new things that Jeroboam created or established.

    _____

    _____

    _____

ISRAEL DIVIDES INTO TWO KINGDOMS
Project 2, Page 2

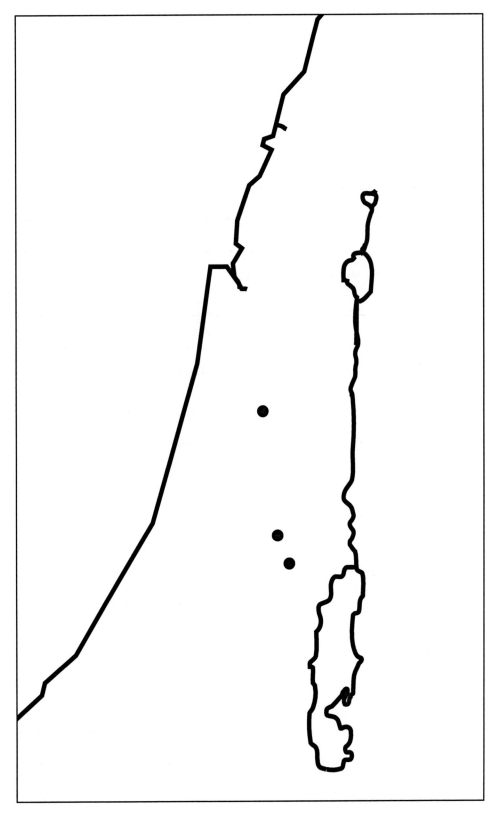

Mediterranean Sea

Samaria

Dan

Bethel

Jerusalem

Northern Kingdom

Southern Kingdom

Israel

Judah

Rehoboam

Jeroboam

Northern capital

Southern capital

ISRAEL DIVIDES INTO TWO KINGDOMS
Test

1. What is the Scripture reference and date for Israel Divides into Two Kingdoms?

   _____

   _____

2. Solomon angered God by building _____.

3. What did God tell Solomon that his punishment would be?

   _____

   _____

   _____

4. How did God's love for David affect Solomon's punishment?

   _____

   _____

5. Who was the prophet that told Jeroboam that he would rule some of the tribes of Israel?

   _____

   _____

6. Jeroboam was Solomon's _____.

   Rehoboam was Solomon's _____.

7. Why did Israel rebel against Solomon's son?

   _____

   _____

   _____

8. How many tribes did Jeroboam rule?

   _____

   _____

   _____

ISRAEL DIVIDES INTO TWO KINGDOMS
Test, Page 2

Review

1. _____ was David's close friend as well as Saul's _____.

2. What was Michal's sin?

   _____

   _____

   _____

3. How did Uriah die?

   _____

   _____

   _____

4. What was Hushai's bad advice to Absalom?

   _____

   _____

   _____

5. What is man's greatest goal in life according to Ecclesiastes?

   _____

   _____

6. List all of the titles, Scripture references, and dates studied so far.

   _____

   _____

   _____

   _____

   _____

ISRAEL DIVIDES INTO TWO KINGDOMS
Test, Page 3

6. (continued)

_____

_____

_____

_____

_____

_____

_____

_____

_____

_____

_____

_____

_____

_____

_____

_____

_____

_____

_____

_____

_____

_____

KINGS OF ISRAEL
Worksheet

1. What is the Scripture reference and date for the Kings of Israel?

   _____

   _____

2. How many tribes did the kings of Israel rule?

   _____

   _____

3. In what region of the old unified Israel did the kings of the divided Israel rule?

   _____

   _____

4. How was Israel less faithful than Judah? What was the consequence of Israel's
   unfaithfulness in this area?

   _____

   _____

   _____

   _____

   _____

5. Who was the first king of Israel after the division?

   _____

   _____

6. How righteous were the kings of Israel?

   _____

   _____

KINGS OF ISRAEL
Worksheet, Page 2

7. What is tribute?

_____

_____

_____

_____

8. What nation conquered Israel?

_____

_____

9. Name one evidence that the nation was weak close to the time when it fell.

_____

_____

_____

_____

THE KINGS OF ISRAEL
Project 1—Bible Reading

In I Kings 15:33–16:34 you will read about the reigns of four kings of Israel. All of these kings are wicked. Watch for a phrase that God uses over and over to describe them as evil. (Hint: He compares the wicked king to another wicked king.) Write the name of the king of Israel that fits each description.

1. Burned the king's house down upon himself _____

2. Was drunk when he was killed _____

3. Moved the capital to Samaria _____

4. Killed all of the house of Baasha _____

5. Was told that dogs or birds would eat his family

   when they died _____

6. Built the city of Samaria _____

7. Was visited by Jehu the prophet _____

8. Half of the people followed Tibni instead of him _____

9. What phrase commonly describes wicked kings? (I Kings 15:34, 16:19, 16:26)

   _____

   _____

   _____

THE KINGS OF ISRAEL
Project 2

Complete the chart listing the reigns of the kings of Israel. Inside each box is the Scripture reference in which you will find the lengths of their reigns and whether they were good or bad kings. If the king was good put a + (plus) in the box. If the king was bad, put a - (minus) in the box. Write the length of the reign in the box.

King	Length of Reign		Good or Bad (+ or -)	
Jeroboam	I Kings 14:20		I Kings 14:7,8	
Nadab	I Kings 15:25		I Kings 15:26	
Baasha	I Kings 15:33		I Kings 15:34	
Elah	I Kings 16:8		I Kings 16:13	
Zimri	I Kings 16:15		I Kings 16:19	
Omri	I Kings 16:23		I Kings 16:25	
Ahab	I Kings 16:29		I Kings 16:30	
Ahaziah	I Kings 22:51		I Kings 22:52	
Joram	II Kings 3:1		II Kings 3:2	
Jehu	II Kings 10:36			
Jehoahaz	II Kings 13:1		II Kings 13:2	
Jehoash	II Kings 13:10		II Kings 13:11	
Jeroboam II	II Kings 14:23		II Kings 14:24	
Zechariah	II Kings 15:8		II Kings 15:9	
Shallum	II Kings 15:13			
Menahem	II Kings 15:17		II Kings 15:18	
Pekahiah	II Kings 15:23		II Kings 15:24	
Pekah	II Kings 15:27		II Kings 15:28	
Hoshea	II Kings 17:1		II Kings 17:2	

What do you notice about the good and bad column?

_____

_____

_____

_____

_____

KINGS OF ISRAEL
Test

1. What is the Scripture reference and date for the Kings of Israel?

   _____

   _____

2. The kings of Israel ruled _____ tribes in the _____

   region of the old unified Israel.

3. Describe Israel's faithfulness to God's command to destroy the Canaanites living
   in the promised land.

   _____

   _____

   _____

   _____

   _____

4. _____ was divided Israel's first king. He was Solomon's _____.

5. For what was Hoshea known?

   _____

   _____

6. What nation conquered Israel?

   _____

   _____

7. The reigns of the final kings were _____ in length and more than

   one man claimed _____.

KINGS OF ISRAEL
Test, Page 2

Review

1. Name the judge connected to each phrase

    _____ the first judge

    _____ the last judge

    _____ sent away soldiers that knelt to drink

    _____ a woman judge

    _____ asked God to make fleece wet and the ground dry

    _____ vowed to sacrifice the first thing that came out of his house

2. Give two points of description about the temple.

    _____

    _____

    _____

3. List all of the titles, Scripture references, and dates studied so far.

    _____

    _____

    _____

    _____

    _____

    _____

    _____

    _____

    _____

    _____

    _____

3. (continued)

_____

_____

_____

_____

_____

_____

_____

_____

_____

_____

_____

_____

_____

_____

_____

_____

_____

_____

_____

_____

_____

KINGS OF JUDAH
Worksheet

1. What is the Scripture reference and date for the Kings of Judah?

   _____

   _____

2. Who was the first king of Judah after it split with Israel?

   _____

   _____

3. Why did the people rebel against their first king?

   _____

   _____

   _____

   _____

4. To whom was the first king related?

   _____

   _____

5. Which two tribes were ruled by the kings of Judah?

   _____

   _____

6. What happened during Asa's reign? Why?

   _____

   _____

   _____

   _____

   _____

   _____

KINGS OF JUDAH
Worksheet, Page 2

7. Why did God put off his judgment on Judah for a time?

_____

_____

_____

_____

8. God was gracious on Judah to grant _____ reigns to the righteous kings.

9. What nation conquered Judah?

_____

_____

THE KINGS OF JUDAH
Project 1—Bible Reading

Read about the lives of two of the kings of Judah. Then under the heading of Good and Bad list some of the good and bad things that each king did.

Asa: II Chronicles 14-16

	GOOD		*BAD*
1.	_____	1.	_____
	_____		_____
2.	_____	2.	_____
	_____		_____
3.	_____	3.	_____
	_____		

Azariah (also called Uzziah): *II Chronicles 26*

	GOOD		*BAD*
1.	_____	1.	_____
	_____		_____
2.	_____	2.	_____
	_____		_____

THE KINGS OF JUDAH
Project 2

Complete the chart listing the reigns of the kings of Judah. Inside each box is a Scripture reference in which you will find the length of their reign and whether they were good or bad kings. If the king was good, put a + (plus) in the box. If the king was bad, put a - (minus) in the box. Write the length of the reign in the box.

King	Length of Reign		Good or Bad (+ or -)	
Rehoboam	I Kings 14:21		I Kings 14:22	
Abijam	I Kings 15:2		I Kings 15:3	
Asa	I Kings 15:9		I Kings 15:11	
Jehoshaphat	I Kings 22:42		I Kings 22:43	
Jehoram	II Kings 8:17		II Kings 8:18, 19	
Ahaziah	II Kings 8:26		II Kings 8:27	
Athaliah	II Kings 11:3		II Kings 11:1	
Joash	II Kings 12:1		II Kings 12:2	
Amaziah	II Kings 14:2		II Kings 14:3	
Azariah	II Kings 15:2		II Kings 15:3	
Jotham	II Kings 15:33		II Kings 15:34	
Ahaz	II Kings 16:2		II Kings 16:2	
Hezekiah	II Kings 18:2		II Kings 18:3	
Manasseh	II Kings 21:1		II Kings 21:2	
Amon	II Kings 21:19		II Kings 21:20	
Josiah	II Kings 21:1		II Kings 21:2	
Jehoahaz	II Kings 23:31		II Kings 23:32	
Jehoiakim	II Kings 23:36		II Kings 23:37	
Jehoiachin	II Kings 24:8		II Kings 24:9	
Zedekiah	II Kings 24:18		II Kings 24:19	

Highlight the rows of the good kings with a highlighter.

Were there more good kings or bad?

_____

What is the total length of time that good kings reigned?

_____

What is the total length of time that bad kings reigned?

_____

KINGS OF JUDAH
Test

1. What is the Scripture reference and date for the Kings of Judah?

   _____

   _____

2. List two things about Rehoboam.

   _____

   _____

   _____

3. How many tribes did the kings of Judah rule? Name them.

   _____

   _____

   _____

   _____

4. Why did some Israelites living near Judah join the Southern Kingdom?

   _____

   _____

   _____

   _____

5. Why did God put off his judgment on Judah for a time?

   _____

   _____

   _____

KINGS OF JUDAH
Test, Page 2

6. What did God do for the righteous kings of Judah which kept Judah from falling sooner?

_____

_____

_____

_____

_____

7. What nation conquered Judah?

_____

_____

Review

1. Name the king that goes with each phrase.

_____ committed adultery and then killed to hide his sin

_____ was hiding in the baggage when he was named king

_____ built the temple

_____ captured Mt. Zion to build his capital city

_____ brought the Ark back to Jerusalem

_____ disobeyed God by not killing all the animals of the enemy

_____ many foreign nobles visited him to see his wealth and wisdom

2. Who tried to steal the kingdom away from David by first giving attention to those who came to see David and then later crowning himself king?

_____

_____

_____

3. List all of the titles, Scripture references, and dates studied so far.

_____

_____

_____

_____

_____

_____

_____

_____

_____

_____

_____

_____

_____

_____

_____

_____

_____

KING OF JUDAH.

3. (continued)

_____

_____

_____

_____

_____

_____

_____

_____

_____

_____

_____

MEMORY VERSES

The following is a listing of some suggested verses for memorization along with the card with which each would correspond. This list is purely supplemental and should be included as the teacher sees fit. The program contains enough without additional memory verses for most learning situations.

NAOMI AND RUTH
Ruth 1:16

SAMUEL, THE LAST JUDGE OF ISRAEL
Judges 21:25

DAVID AND GOLIATH
I Samuel 17:45–47

DAVIDIC KINGDOM
II Samuel 7:16

JONATHAN PROTECTS DAVID
Psalm 18:1–3

CONQUEST OF JERUSALEM
Psalm 24

DAVID WRITES MANY PSALMS (OR ANY CARD)
Psalm 8:3–5 (or whole chapter)/Psalm 15:1–3/Psalm 19:7–10/Psalm 103/Psalm 119:105

DAVID AND BATHSHEBA
Psalm 51

SOLOMON WRITES PROVERBS AND ECCLESIASTES
Ecclesiastes 3:1–4/Proverbs 3:5, 6/Proverbs 3:11, 12/Proverbs 9:10/Proverbs 13:20/Proverbs 29:22, 23

THE END OF SOLOMON'S REIGN
I Kings 11:11–12

JUDGES THROUGH KINGS
Song Lyrics

We will continue with our practice
Of the chronologic order
Of the Scriptures as they all were written down
So come and follow 'long this pathway
As we memorize this mapping
Of the stories in the Bible as they're found

First the Judges of Israel came in Judges chapter One
Around the time of thirteen hundred eighty-nine
They continued to help Israel when they'd got themselves in trouble
Till ten hundred fifty way back in time

Othniel and Ehud were sent in Judges chapter three
To save Israel from their enemies
Between the years of thirteen hundred seventy-seven
And thirteen hundred thirty-seven you got it B.C.

Now Deborah was a prophetess who brought a great deliverance
In Judges chapter four and Judges chapter five
Way back in thirteen hundred fifty and still there's something nifty
In the next event of that Bible time

Oh, Gideon delivered Israel in 1350 B.C.
Found in Judges chapter six read about his fleece
Then Jephthah rescued Israel round that same old year
In Judges chapter eleven and twelve he sacrificed his dear sweet daughter

We will continue with our practice
Of the chronologic order
Of the Scriptures as they all were written down
So come and follow 'long this pathway
As we memorize this mapping
Of the stories in the Bible as they're found

Naomi counseled Ruth into marrying Boaz
Round in eleven hundred in her book chapters one through four
Then Samson married a Philistine in Judges thirteen through sixteen
Her name Delilah in 1080 B.C., you want more!

Hannah and the high priest Eli, met with one another
While she's praying that, she could have a son
In ten hundred seventy-five B.C. the Lord gives her, her wish you see
In chapters one and two of Samuel one

JUDGES THROUGH KINGS
Song Lyrics

Samuel now becomes the last Judge of Israel's ancient past
The year's ten hundred sixty five B.C.
In First Samuel one and two He's obedient from his youth
And he serves the Lord so very faithfully

The Ark of the Covenant of Israel was taken into captivity
In First Samuel chapters four through six it was stolen by the Philistines
Then came the first King of Israel in First Samuel chapter nine
Saul was anointed by Samuel while looking for his donkeys

Then came the genealogy of David, Jesse's son
Back in the year so old ten hundred and forty-one
You can read the lineage in First Chronicles chapter two
Or read it so much easier in Matthew's Gospel

We will continue with our practice
Of the chronologic order
Of the Scriptures as they all were written down
So come and follow 'long this pathway
As we memorize this mapping
Of the stories in the Bible as they're found

Saul sinned at Amalek his attitude was very sick
Back in chapter fifteen of first Samuel
And because of Saul's rebellion, David is anointed
As the handsome, ruddy King over Israel
From then on Saul was troubled in 1030 B.C.
And in the Book first Samuel chapter sixteen

David and Goliath a midget and a giant
Fought with one another in Chapter seventeen
A stone into the head well it knocked that giant dead
In the year 1028 B.C.
Then Jonathan protected David as his friend
In ten hundred twenty B.C. and in first Samuel chapter twenty

The death of Saul and Jonathan in First Samuel thirty-one
Came around the time of 1011 B.C.
Next the Davidic Kingdom it reigned for forty years
Until the year nine-seven-one B.C.
The stories they are found in Samuel one and two
And in the Bible First Chronicles

Judges through Kings
Song Lyrics

The conquest of Jerusalem in ten-o-three B.C.
Chapter five and the second Book of Samuel
Preceded David's dance and an effort he would chance
When the Ark was enthroned in Jerusalem
It all happened in 1000 B.C.
And in the second book of Samuel chapter six

We will continue with our practice
Of the chronologic order
Of the Scriptures as they all were written down
So come and follow 'long this pathway
As we memorize this mapping
Of the stories in the Biblc as they're found

Now David writes the Psalms so many you can count them they are plenty
Around the year one thousand wrote them all
Then David took Bathsheba to his house and
Committed adultery with the spouse
Of Uriah in second Samuel eleven through twelve

Then in second Samuel fifteen to the end of chapter eighteen
The story about David and Absalom
Then Solomon's Reign in nine hundred seventy-one
Through nine hundred thirty-one in chapters one through eleven in Kings

Solomon's given wisdom in first Kings chapter three
In the year of 970 B.C.
Then he writes many Proverbs and the book of Ecclesiastes
In the year of 970 B.C.

The Temple is Built in first Kings six in nine-seven-o B.C.
Queen Sheba came to Solomon out of her curiosity
She came around to see him in nine-five-o B.C.
And in first Kings ten what she saw surpassed her expectations

We will continue with our practice
Of the chronologic order
Of the Scriptures as they all were written down
So come and follow 'long this pathway
As we memorize this mapping
Of the stories in the Bible as they're found

Judges through Kings
Song Lyrics

The End of Solomon's Reign came in nine-three-one B.C.
In chapter eleven in the first book of Kings
Although his wisdom surpassed many he did not stay faithful
To the laws of God that he had been given

Then in 931 B.C. Israel divides their kingdom
Into two separate countries we are told
And so it's written in First Kings chapter twelve
And likewise in chapter ten of First Chronicles

Now from 931 to 722 the Kings of Israel ruled
Over ten northern tribes and their lands
Then from 931 to 583 B.C. the Kings of Judah ruled
Over the southern Kingdom

We will continue with our practice
Of the chronologic order
Of the Scriptures as they all were written down
So come and follow 'long this pathway
As we memorize this mapping
Of the stories in the Bible as they're found

ANSWERS

THE JUDGES

Worksheet
1. c. 1389–1050 B.C.
2. Failing to destroy all of the Canaanites, idol worship
3. Allowing the Canaanites to oppress them
4. Raise up a judge
5. God
6. Answers will vary.

Project 1
dedi/died
hoajus/Joshua
meniees/enemies
notnais/nations
ddeerlunp/plundered
gujesd/Judges
alabs/Baals

1. Israel served the Lord until Joshua died.
2. The Israelites forsook the Lord and instead served the Baals.
3. God handed Israel over to their enemies.
4. Israel was oppressed and plundered.
5. God raised up judges to deliver them.
6. When the judge died the people became corrupt again.
7. God no longer drove out the nations which remained in the land when Joshua died.

Project 3
1. The Israelites go after idols and forsake the Lord.
2. God punishes Israel by allowing enemies to oppress them.
3. The Israelites cry out to God.
4. God raises up a judge.
5. The Israelites are freed.

Test
1. 1389–1050 B.C.
2. They did not destroy all of the Canaanites.
3. The Israelites sin by following false gods.
   God punishes Israel by allowing Canaanites to oppress them.
   The Israelites finally cry out to God.
   God sends a judge.
   The people are freed.
   But then the Israelites worship idols again.
5. Answers will vary.

OTHNIEL AND EHUD

Worksheet
1. Judges 3; c. 1377–1337 B.C.
2. King of Mesopotamia
3. The first judge
4. King of Moab
5. Ehud came to Eglon saying that he had a secret message from God. Eglon sent out his guards. Ehud struck Eglon in the belly.
6. Ehud escaped and led Israel in defeating the Moabites.

Project 1
Othniel
Israel worships other gods. v. 7
God hands Israel over to its enemies. v. 8
Israel cries out to God. v. 9
God sends a judge. v. 9
Israel is freed. v. 10
Ehud
Israel worships other gods. v. 12
God hands Israel over to its enemies. v. 13
Israel cries out to God. v. 15
God sends a judge. v. 15
Israel is freed. v. 30

Project 2
Othniel and Ehud
Judges 3
I. Othniel
  A. Israel did evil...
  B. Othniel was Israel's first judge
II. Ehud
  A. The Moab king...
  B. Ehud went in to see...

Test
1. Judges 3; c. 1377–1337 B.C.
2. Othniel
3. Eglon
4. He pretended that he had a secret message from God.
5. He struck him in the belly.
6. He escaped and led Israel in defeating the Moabites.

ANSWERS

DEBORAH THE PROPHETESS
Worksheet
1. Judges 4, 5; c. 1350 B.C.
2. Prophetess
3. Commander of Jabin's army
4. Barak, He would go only if Deborah went with him.
5. He would not get the glory for capturing Sisera.
6. Jael
7. She pounded a tent peg through his head.

Project 1
Deborah
    sat under a palm tree
    prophetess
    judge
Barak
    commander of the Israelite army
    would not go by himself
Jabin
    had 900 chariots of iron
    King of Canaan
Jael
    killed Sisera
    called the enemy to her tent
Sisera
    received a drink from his killer
    commander of the enemy army
    ran away on foot

Test
1. Judges 4, 5; c. 1350 B.C.
2. Prophetess
3. Commander of the Israelite army
4. He said he would only go fight if Deborah went with him.
5. Sisera
6. He was fleeing, and he thought she would hide him.
7. By pounding a tent peg through his head

GIDEON DELIVERS ISRAEL
Worksheet
1. Judges 6, 7; c. 1350 B.C.
2. He asked God to make a fleece wet but the ground dry. The next day he wanted the fleece dry and the ground wet.
3. Those who were afraid and those who knelt to drink
4. So Israel would know that it was God who won the battle

5. 300
6. At night
7. They blew trumpets and broke pitchers. The Midianites were confused and attacked and killed each other.

Project 1
I. A. father, Baal, worshiped
        1. Tear it down
        2. at night, his father's household and the men of the city
  B. torn down
        1. kill him
        2. father, deal with him
II.
  A. sign
        1. wet, dry, is behind him
        2. fleece, wet, ground, dry, fleece, dry, ground, wet, does
  B.
        2. Men
          a. afraid
          b. got down on their knees to drink water
        3. 300
  C. Midianites
        1. trumpets, pitchers, torches
        2. fled
        3. destroyed them

Test
1. Judges 6, 7; c. 1350 B.C.
2. Gideon put a fleece on the ground at night. In the morning the ground was dry and the fleece was wet.
3. Those who were afraid and those who knelt to drink
4. So Israel would know that it was God who won the battle
5. 300
6. At night
7. They blew trumpets and broke pitchers. The Midianites were confused and attacked and killed each other.

Review
1. Answers will vary.
2. The first judge
3. Commander of Jabin's army
4. Jael's

ANSWERS

JEPHTHAH'S FOOLISH VOW
Worksheet
1. Judges 11, 12; c. 1350 B.C.
2. The Ammonites
3. The Ephraimites were angry because the Gileadites received all the glory and spoils from the victory over the Ammonites.
4. The Gileadites
5. They made those fleeing say a word that the Ephraimites couldn't pronounce.
6. He would sacrifice the first thing that came out of his house if God gave him victory.
7. His daughter came out to greet him.
8. It died out.

Project 1
I.
    A. Gilead
    B. harlot
    C. from his father's house
II.
    A. messengers, Ammonites, land, Israel, Ammonite
    B. vowed, sacrifice, out of his house when he returned home
    C. victory
    D. daughter
        3. two months, mourn, friends, got married
III. The Ephraimites
    A. fight, Gideon
    B.
        1. defeated
        2. Ephraimites, river, their land, Shibboleth
            a. pronounce, Shibboleth
            b. killed, Sibboleth, Shibboleth

Test
1. Judges 11, 12; c. 1350 B.C.
2. The Gileadites
3. The Ephraimites were angry because the Gileadites received all of the glory and spoils from the victory over the Ammonites. They had not been willing to fight against the Ammonites.
4. They made those fleeing say a word that the Ephraimites couldn't pronounce.
5. He would sacrifice the first thing that came out of his house if God gave him victory.
6. His daughter came out to greet him.
7. She may have been sacrificed or she may have had to serve all her life in the sanctuary.

Review
1. To free the people from oppression
2. The king of Moab that Ehud killed
3. Drove a tent peg through his head
4. Commander of the Israelite army
5. 300

NAOMI AND RUTH
Worksheet
1. Ruth 1–4; c. 1100 B.c.
2. Naomi was Ruth's mother-in-law
3. Back to Israel
4. Bitter
5. Boaz
6. She lay down at his feet while he was sleeping.
7. The closest relative to Ruth
8. David is their great-grandson. Jesus is the most famous relative.
9. Avenge enemies and care for widows

Project 1
I.
    A. Moab, sons, Moabite, husband
    B. Moabite, Naomi's, Naomi
    C. relative
II.
    A. foreign
    B. Israel, food, Ruth
III.
    A. Ruth
        1. eat, drink
        2. grain
    B. Naomi, Boaz's feet
    C.
        1.
        2. relative, marrying
        3. man, witnesses, field, Naomi, Ruth
        4. sandal, gave, settled
        5. Boaz, Ruth, son
    D. Boaz, Ruth, Obed, grandfather

Project 2
PLOWING & SOWING: Plowing is the process . . .
HARVEST: The farmer used a sickle, a sharp curved . . .
THRESHING: Threshing is beating or crushing . . .
WINNOWING: Once the grain was separated from . . .
STORAGE: The good grain was stored in great . . .

ANSWERS

Test
1. Ruth 1–4; c. 1100 B.C.
2. Naomi was Ruth's mother-in-law
3. Moab
4. Mara
5. Boaz
6. She lay down at his feet while he was sleeping. Boaz then got Ruth's closest relative to give up the right to marry her.
7. David and Jesus
8. The law of the kinsman-redeemer

Review
1. Not destroying the Canaanites, idol worship
2. Ehud pretended to have a secret message from God, so Eglon sent the guards out of the room. Then Ehud struck Eglon in the belly with a dagger.
3. Barak
4. He asked God to make a fleece wet but the ground dry. The next day, he wanted the fleece dry and the ground wet.
5. See the master list on page 274.

SAMSON AND DELILAH
Worksheet
1. Judges 13–16; c. 1080 B.C.
2. Philistines
3. His mother had been unable to have children.
4. Drink strong drink or cut his hair
5. Jawbone of an ass
6. Delilah
7. He never cut his hair.
8. Delilah enticed him to tell her the secret of his strength. While he slept, she cut his hair so he became weak. The Philistines came in, captured him, and put out his eyes.
9. At a big gathering they brought him out to mock him and his God. He was given his strength back, and he knocked down the pillars holding up the building.

Project 2
Othniel
  Judges 3
  was the first judge
Ehud
  Judges 3
  was left-handed
  killed King Eglon
  got in to see the king by saying that he had a secret message from God

Deborah
  Judges 4–5
  was also a prophetess
  prophesied that the glory of victory would go to a woman
  helped Barak defeat the Canaanites
  fought against Sisera
Gideon
  Judges 6–7
  sent away those who were afraid and lapped water like a dog
  went into battle with only 300 men
  asked God to make the fleece wet and the ground dry
  tore down the altars of Baal at his father's house at night
Jephthah
  Judges 11–12
  vowed to sacrifice the first thing that came out of his house
  chased out of town by his brothers
  made the Ephramites say Shibboleth
  gave his daughter two months to weep with her friends
  his line died out
Samson
  Judges 13–16
  killed 1000 Philistines with a donkey's jawbone
  was a Nazarite
  tied the tails of foxes together and let them loose in the Philistines' fields
  killed more of God's enemies in his death by pushing down the pillars that held up a building
  eyes were poked out
  the secret to his strength was to not cut his hair
  mother wasn't able to have children without God's help
  told a riddle about a lion and honey at his wedding

Project 3
1. Philistines
2. To keep Samson from getting away.
To draw your eye into the action.
3. Fear and/or victory
4. The weapons, armor and clothing

ANSWERS

Test
1. Judges 13–16; c. 1080 B.C.
2. Philistines
3. She would have a son who would be a Nazarite.
4. Drink strong drink or cut his hair
5. Incredible strength
6. With a jawbone of an ass he killed a thousand Philistines.
7. Delilah enticed him to tell her the secret of his strength. While he slept, she cut his hair so he became weak. The Philistines came in, captured him, and put his eyes out.
8. At a big gathering they brought him out to mock him and his God. He was given his strength back, and he knocked down the pillars holding up the building.

Review
1. Ehud
2. The glory of capturing Sisera would go to someone else.
3. They blew trumpets and broke pitchers. The Midianites were confused and killed each other.
4. It died out.
5. See the master list on page 274.

HANNAH AND ELI
Worksheet
1. I Samuel 1–2; c. 1075 B.C.
2. Offer sacrifices to God
3. She could not have children. Peninnah
4. Eat. She went to the tabernacle to pray.
5. The High Priest
6. If she had a child, she would give him to serve in the tabernacle.
7. He thought she was drunk.
8. Samuel
9. After he was weaned

Project

```
H A N N A A H E L K A N N A H V
E O W E A N E D N E D B U S T A
P V R D A L P H P S W O R D E L
T W A D H R A Z E R W E A N E O
W E A N E A C H I L O L E S S U
T S D R O N N R T Y U V O W I C
E A S E L I C N V B N M O P O H
L M B S L S C X A Z X C V K N I
K U V E S K V B N H G H J K E L
A E V P R S A W E R L G W D A D
N L E R A N S N S U K R O R M L
A P R E Z L A S A T J A R U O E
S A I S O E M C S H C K N E S S
D O T S R S A K L S Y E S K L S
G L A G U L F J W E P T F G H J
H N S H Y I G H B I B L E A B C
```

Test
1. I Samuel 1–2; c. 1075 B.C.
2. Elkanah
3. Peninnah was another wife of Elkanah, and she berated Hannah.
4. to pray
5. The High Priest
6. If she had a child, she would give him to serve in the tabernacle.
7. He thought she was drunk.
8. He told her that God would answer her prayer.
9. Samuel was born.

Review
1. Prophetess
2. Jael
3. So they would know it was God who earned the victory.
4. He would sacrifice the first thing that came out of his house if God would give him victory.
5. Boaz
6. See the master list on page 274.

ANSWERS

SAMUEL, THE LAST JUDGE OF ISRAEL
Worksheet
1. I Samuel 2–4; c. 1065 B.C.
2. They provoked God's people, stole from the sacrifices, and committed immorality with the women who served in the tabernacle.
3. At night the Lord called Samuel, but he thought it was Eli calling. After three times Eli realized it was God, so Samuel talked to God.
4. God would destroy Eli's family.
5. Samuel saw the rise and fall of Saul, and he anointed David as king of Israel.

Project 1
1. Take a poke at the meat while it was boiling with a three-pronged fleshhook
2. They demanded to take their share while it was raw and not boiled.
3. He didn't restrain his sons from their wickedness.
4. He was afraid to tell Eli.
5. He was content. He said, "Let Him do what seems good to Him."

Project 2
Othniel—enslaved 8 years—40 years freedom
Ehud—enslaved 18 years—80 years freedom
Deborah—enslaved 20 years—40 years freedom
Gideon—enslaved 7 years—40 years freedom
Jephthah—enslaved 18 years—6 years freedom
Samson—enslaved 40 years—20 years freedom
1. Years of enslavement lengthened
2. Years of freedom shortened
3. Their lengths get closer together

Test
1. I Samuel 2–4; c. 1065 B.C.
2. Hophni and Phinehas
3. They provoked God's people, stole from the sacrifices, and committed immorality with the women who served in the tabernacle.
4. The Lord called Samuel, but he thought it was Eli calling.
5. three times
6. God would destroy Eli's family.
7. Samuel saw the rise and fall of Saul, and he anointed David as king of Israel.

Review
1. Othniel
2. He would go only if Deborah went with him.
3. He got rid of those who were afraid or knelt to drink.
4. His daughter
5. Ruth's closest relative
6. See the master list on page 274.

THE ARK IS TAKEN INTO CAPTIVITY
Worksheet
1. I Samuel 4–6; c. 1050 B.C.
2. They thought that would make God give them victory.
3. The Ark was captured, and Eli's sons died.
4. He fell over backwards after hearing about the Ark.
5. The Philistines
6. At the temple of Dagon they set the Ark first. In the morning the statue of Dagon was face down in front of the Ark. They put it back up, but the next morning it was lying before the Ark with its head and hands broken off.
7. Plagues of rats and tumors broke out.
8. They put it on a cart hitched to cows and let them go where they wanted. The cows pulled it straight back to Israel.

Project 1
Articles
the/a
Nouns
Philistines/ark/Hophni/Dagon/tumors/cart/cows
Verbs
captured/died/fell/hitched
Adjectives
wicked/five/golden/two/milk
Adverbs
backwards/finally

Project 3
1. The Philistines defeated the Israelites in battle on the first two days.
2. The Israelites took the Ark into battle because they thought God would give them victory.
3. Hophni and Phinehas were killed and the Ark was captured.
4. Eli fell over backwards and died.
5. The Philistines put the Ark in the temple of their god, Dagon.
6. Dagon was found lying face down before the Ark.
7. They set Dagon back up.
8. Dagon was lying before the Ark with its head

ANSWERS

and hands broken off.

9. The Philistines moved the Ark out of the temple of Dagon and into another city.
10. God sent plagues of rats and tumors on the cities where the Ark was kept.
11. The Ark was put on a cart and hitched to cows.
12. The cows pulled the cart with the Ark straight back to Israel.

Test
1. I Samuel 4–6; c. 1050 B.C.
2. Eli's sons died.
3. The Philistines
4. When he heard about the Ark being captured, he fell over backwards and died.
5. In the morning the statue of Dagon was face down in front of the Ark. They put it back up, but the next morning it was lying before the Ark with its head and hands broken off.
6. Plagues of rats and tumors broke out.
7. They put it on a cart hitched to cows, and let them go where they wanted. The cows pulled it straight back to Israel.

Review
1. Eglon
2. Deborah
3. Avenge enemies and protect widows
4. Samuel
5. At night God called Samuel, but he thought it was Eli. After the third time of confusion, Eli realized God must be calling Samuel, so he told Samuel to ask the Lord to speak to him.
6. See the master list on page 274.

SAUL, THE FIRST KING OF ISRAEL
Worksheet
1. I Samuel 9, 10; c. 1043 B.C.
2. Samuel's sons
3. They were wicked. They took bribes and were unfair.
4. They wanted a king instead.
5. The problems a king would cause
6. Saul
7. Looking for his father's donkeys
8. He gathered all of Israel together. He narrowed down the Israelites by tribe, clan, and family.
9. Hiding behind the baggage

Project 1
1. Benjamin
2. handsome
3. father's
4. shekel
5. sacrifice, high place
6. flask
7. prophets
8. baggage
9. royalty

Test
1. I Samuel 9, 10; c. 1043 B.C.
2. Samuel's sons
3. They were wicked. They took bribes and were unfair.
4. Israel wanted a king so they could be like the other nations.
5. Take their daughters as servants, sons for his army, and crops for himself
6. his father's donkeys
7. They put it on a cart hitched to cows, and let
8. When Samuel announced the new king he gathered together all of Israel and then narrowed it down by tribe, clan, and family until he finally came to Saul.
9. Hiding behind the baggage

Review
1. Raised up judges
2. Naomi was Ruth's mother-in-law
3. His mother had been unable to have children.
4. He pushed over the pillars of a building killing thousands of Philistines.
5. Peninnah
6. Eli's family would be destroyed.
7. See the master list on page 274.

THE GENEALOGY OF DAVID
Worksheet
1. I Chronicles 2; c. 1041 B.C.
2. Abraham, Isaac, Jacob, Judah, Perez, Hezron, Ram, Amminadab, Nahshon, Salmon, Boaz, Obed, Jesse, David
3. Abraham
4. His parents were too old to have children.
5. That he was the one to raise up Israel
6. The twelve tribes of Israel
7. They were the strongest militarily and spiritually.
8. Boaz
9. Obed
10. 8
11. David

ANSWERS

Project 1

Er
Onan
Shelah
Zerah
Perez

Zimri
Ethan
Heman
Calcol
Dara
Hezron
Hamul

Jerahmeel
Ram
Chelubai

Amminadab
Nahshon
Salmon
Boaz
Obed
Jesse

Eliab
Abinadab
Shimea
Nethanel
Raddai
Ozem
David

Test

1. I Chronicles 2; c. 1041 B.C.
2. Abraham, Isaac, Jacob, Judah, Perez, Hezron, Ram, Amminadab, Nahshon, Salmon, Boaz, Obed, Jesse, David
3. Judah
4. Boaz
5. The heads of the twelve tribes of Israel
6. Abraham
7. David
8. Obed
9. 8
10. His parents were too old to have children.

Review

1. Jesus
2. The Israelites sin by forsaking God and worshiping idols.
   God punishes Israel by allowing another country to oppress them.
   The Israelites finally cry out to God.
   God sends a judge.
   The people are freed.
   But then the Israelites turn back to idols.
3. See the master list on page 274.

SAUL'S SIN AT AMALEK

Worksheet

1. I Samuel 15; c. 1032 B.C.
2. God commanded Saul to kill every person and every animal of the Amalekites.
3. He spared King Agag and kept the best of the king's animals.
4. He said he had obeyed the Lord's command.
5. The soldiers
6. Sacrifice them
7. King of the Amalekites
8. God rejected him as king.
9. Saul had previously sinned by not waiting for Samuel to offer the sacrifice before battle.

Project

Test

1. I Samuel 15; c. 1032 B.C.
2. God commanded Saul to kill every person and every animal of the Amalekites.
3. He spared King Agag and kept the best of the king's animals.
4. The soldiers
5. Sacrifice them
6. Agag
7. God rejected him as king.
8. Saul had previously sinned by not waiting for Samuel to offer the sacrifice before battle.

ANSWERS

Review
1. Destroy them
2. Bitter, Naomi
3. Delilah
4. He fell over backwards.
5. He gathered together all of Israel. Then he narrowed it down by tribe, clan, and family.
6. See the master list on page 274.

DAVID IS ANOINTED AS KING

Worksheet
1. I Samuel 16; c. 1030 B.C.
2. The king will be one of Jesse's sons.
3. He says he is going to make a sacrifice in Bethlehem.
4. He was tall and handsome.
5. Do you have any more sons?
6. Tending the sheep
7. The Spirit of the Lord left Saul, and an evil spirit was sent by God to distress him.
8. Get a harp player
9. David
10. He made him his armor bearer.

Project 1
heifer—a heifer to sacrifice
harp—harp player
horn—horn with oil
armor bearer—became his armor bearer
heart—looks at the heart
depart—the spirit would depart
sheep—tending sheep
distressing—distressing spirit

Project 2
1. v. 4
3. v. 2
4. v. 4
6. v. 2
8. v. 2, 3
10. v. 1

Test
1. I Samuel 16; c. 1030 B.C.
2. Jesse
3. He was afraid Saul would kill him if he found out what Samuel was doing.
4. He was tall and handsome.
5. Tending the sheep.
6. He was handsome and ruddy.

7. The Spirit of the Lord left Saul, and an evil spirit was sent by God to distress him.
8. Get a harp player
9. He made him his armor bearer.

Review
1. She was sacrificed or made to serve in the temple.
2. She lay down at his feet while he was sleeping.
3. If God would grant her a child, she would give him to serve in the tabernacle.
4. Eli's sons.
5. Hiding behind the baggage
6. See the master list on page 274.

DAVID AND GOLIATH

Worksheet
1. I Samuel 17; c. 1028 B.C.
2. Israel would send out a champion to fight him. Whichever champion lost, his country would serve the other.
3. 40
4. Philistines
5. David
6. Goliath had mocked God and His people.
7. His armor
8. It wasn't useful, because David couldn't move in it.
9. Sling and stone, sword

Project 1
1. Goliath's mail coat weighed 5,000 shekels.
2. One champion from each army would fight the other.
3. For 40 days Goliath came forth to make his challenge.
4. Jesse had three sons who were with Saul in battle.
5. David was sent to take food to his brothers and ten cheeses to their captain.
6. David fought Goliath with five smooth stones.
7. David had no sword so he used Goliath's sword to cut off his head.

Project 2
1. No, chiaroscuro is used to add drama to the scene and focus our attention on the main characters.
2. Light is falling on David while Goliath's head is shrouded more in shadows.
3. Caravaggio's painting—David was a young man but also an established warrior and talented musician.

ANSWERS

Test
1. I Samuel 17; c. 1028 B.C.
2. Philistines
3. Israel would send out a champion to fight him. Whichever champion lost, his country would serve the other.
4. 40
5. Food
6. Killing lions and bears to protect his sheep
7. His armor
8. It wasn't useful, because David couldn't move in it.
9. David used a sling and stone to knock him down and then cut his head off with his own sword.

Review
1. He made the fleece wet and the ground dry. Then he made the fleece dry and the ground wet.
2. His uncut hair
3. Provoked God's people, stole from the sacrifices, and committed immorality with the women who served in the tabernacle
4. They put it on a cart pulled by two cows. The cows pulled it back to Israel with no one directing them.
5. Wicked
6. The soldiers
7. See the master list on page 274.

JONATHAN PROTECTS DAVID
Worksheet
1. I Samuel 20; c. 1020 B.C.
2. He had defeated Goliath.
3. He saw that David had God's blessing and power.
4. Jonathan was Saul's son.
5. They were best friends.
6. It was dangerous for Jonathan to be seen with David.
7. New moon festival
8. Jonathan shot arrows and sent his servant after them. How he described where the arrows were would let David know if he was safe or in danger.
9. Run for his life

Test
1. I Samuel 20; c. 1020 B.C.
2. He had defeated Goliath.
3. He saw that David had God's blessing and power.
4. Jonathan was Saul's son.
5. They were best friends.
6. If David was safe or in danger

7. Jonathan pretended to be practicing shooting arrows. David was hiding in a nearby field.
8. By calling to the boy that the arrows were behind him, Jonathan let David know he should run for his life.

Review
1. They made everyone say a word that the Ephraimites could not pronounce.
2. He thought she was drunk.
3. Take their daughters for servants, sons for his army, and crops for himself
4. He gathered all of Israel together. Then he narrowed them down by tribe, clan, and family until he came to Saul.
5. The twelve tribes of Israel
6. God rejected him as king.
7. See the master list on page 274.

THE DEATHS OF SAUL AND JONATHAN
Worksheet
1. I Samuel 31; c. 1011 B.C.
2. He would not raise his hand against the Lord's anointed.
3. In a Philistine city
4. By an arrow
5. To pierce him with his sword
6. He fell on his own sword.
7. Jonathan
8. David had him killed.
9. "The Song of the Bow"

Project 1
1. David had the chance to kill Saul, but he refused to raise his hand against the Lord's anointed. Instead he took a spear and jug of water next to Saul.
2. David killed the soldier who claimed to have killed Saul. He did not think anyone but God should end Saul's life.
3. David wrote the "Song of the Bow" lamenting Saul (and Jonathan's) death. He told Israel to teach their children the song to always honor Saul.

Test
1. I Samuel 31; c. 1011 B.C.
2. He would not raise his hand against the Lord's anointed.
3. In a Philistine city

ANSWERS

4. Saul was wounded by an arrow and asked his armor bearer to kill him. The armor bearer refused, so Saul fell on his own sword.
5. Jonathan
6. He said he had killed Saul.
7. David had him killed because he dared to touch the Lord's anointed.
8. "The Song of the Bow" is a song written by David lamenting the deaths of Saul and Jonathan.

Review
1. They thought it would cause God to help them win the battle.
2. His sons
3. He was tall and handsome.
4. Judah
5. Tending the sheep
6. Israel should send out a champion. Whichever champion lost, his country would serve the other.
7. See the master list on page 274.

DAVIDIC KINGDOM
Worksheet
1. I & II Samuel, I Chronicles; c. 1011–971 B.C.
2. Bethlehem
3. Killing Goliath
4. The people cheered more for David than for him.
5. Live as an outlaw
6. 40 years
7. David was the second and most prominent king of Israel.

Test
1. I & II Samuel, I Chronicles; c. 1011–971 B.C.
2. Jesse
3. Killing Goliath
4. Saul became jealous and wanted to kill him.
5. Saul was trying to kill him.
6. Saul's death
7. 40 years
8. David is known as the most prominent king of Israel.

Review
1. The first judge
2. Give him to serve in the tabernacle
3. Saul
4. Abraham
5. God commanded Saul to kill every person and every animal of the Amalekites.
6. He was jealous and saw David had God's blessing.
7. See the master list on page 274.

THE CONQUEST OF JERUSALEM
Worksheet
1. II Samuel 5; c. 1003 B.C.
2. Ish-Bosheth
3. Judah supported David. Most of the rest of Israel supported Ish-Bosheth.
4. Ish-Bosheth died.
5. The Jebusites
6. His men entered through the water supply.
7. Mt. Zion
8. Cedar trees, carpenters, and stone masons
9. For the exaltation of His people

Project 1
answers will vary

Test
1. II Samuel 5; c. 1003 B.C.
2. Ish-Bosheth was Saul's son who claimed to be king when Saul died.
3. Judah supported David. Most of the rest of Israel supported Ish-Bosheth.
4. Ish-Bosheth died.
5. The Jebusites occupied the city of Jebus which David wanted as a stronghold.
6. His men entered through the water supply.
7. Mt. Zion was the mountain on which Jerusalem is built.
8. The king of Tyre, to build Jerusalem
9. For the exaltation of His people

Review
1. Delilah cut his hair.
2. Plagues of rats and tumors broke out.
3. David
4. Played his harp
5. He could not move in it.
6. He shot arrows in the field. By calling to his servant that the arrows were behind him, Jonathan let David know he should run for his life.
7. See the master list on page 274.

THE ARK ENTHRONED IN JERUSALEM
Worksheet
1. II Samuel 6; c. 1000 B.C.
2. The Levites were to carry it.
3. They put it on an ox-drawn cart like the Philistines did.
4. He reached out to steady the Ark. He was struck dead.
5. He blessed it while the Ark was there.

ANSWERS

6. Every six paces he made a sacrifice.
7. He was dancing before the Lord.
8. Michal, She was unable to have children.

Project 1

Project 2
1. Righteous
2. Sinful
3. Righteous
4. Righteous
5. Sinful
6. Righteous
7. Righteous
8. Sinful
9. Righteous

Test
1. II Samuel 6; c. 1000 B.C.
2. The Levites were to carry it.
3. They put it on an ox-drawn cart like the Philistines did.
4. Uzzah. He was struck dead.
5. Every six paces.
6. David
7. Michal was David's wife.
8. She was so proud that she was ashamed of David's humility.

Review
1. Answers will vary.
2. See the master list on page 274.

DAVID WRITES MANY PSALMS
Worksheet
1. David
2. Psalms of lament, confession, praise, thanksgiving, and imprecatory psalms
3. In psalms of lament the author cries out to God for help.
4. Psalm 51
5. Imprecatory psalms call for God to judge his enemies.
6. c. 1000 B.C.

Project 1
Praise Psalm 33 The psalmist praises God's works of creation, ruling the nations and working in the hearts of men.
Thanksgiving Psalm 9 God has destroyed his enemies.
Lament Psalm 88 He wants God to stop forsaking him.
Imprecatory Psalm 129 He asks God to make them like withered grass.
Confession Psalm 38 He is physically weak, his loved ones are far from him and his enemies surround him.

Project 2
THE HERITAGE OF THE RIGHTEOUS
Be given the desires of their heart
Righteousness and justice will be brought forth
Inherit the earth
Be satisfied in days of famine
Future of peace
THE CALAMITY OF THE WICKED
Cut down like grass
Wither as a green herb
Cut off
God laughs at him
Their sword shall enter their own heart
Will perish

Test
1. Psalms of lament, confession, praise, thanksgiving, and imprecatory psalms
2. In psalms of lament the author cries out to God for help.
3. Psalm 51 is a psalm of confession.
4. David's sin with Bathsheba

ANSWERS

5. Imprecatory psalms call for God to judge his enemies.
6. c. 1000 B.C.

Review
1. Eli's family would be destroyed.
2. The Israelites demanded to be ruled by a king so they could be like other nations.
3. Killing lions and bears to protect his sheep
4. That he had killed Saul when really he had not
5. 40 years
6. They put it on an ox-drawn cart.
7. See the master list on page 274.

DAVID AND BATHSHEBA
Worksheet
1. II Samuel 11–12; c. 995 B.C.
2. Adultery
3. Uriah
4. He called Uriah home from the battle. Uriah refused to go home to his wife.
5. Put Uriah on the front line so he would be killed
6. David
7. God's prophet who confronted David with his sin
8. He died.
9. Solomon

Project 1
1. (v. 1) leading his army in war
2. He did not want the comforts of home while his fellow soldiers were at war.
3. (v. 13) got him drunk
4. front line, killed
5. Nathan told of a poor man who had a beloved lamb, and a rich man who had many lambs. The rich man took the poor man's lamb to kill and serve a guest rather than slaughter one of his own sheep. David said the rich man deserved to die. Then Nathan told David that he was the rich man.

Project 2
1. adultery and murder
2. God desires truth on the inside.
3. Snow
4. A clean heart
5. teach transgressors God's ways
6. broken spirit and a contrite heart

Test
1. II Samuel 11–12; c. 995 B.C.
2. Adultery
3. Bathsheba's husband
4. Joab put Uriah on the front line so he would be killed. He was killed to cover up David's sin with Bathsheba.
5. David and Joab
6. David
7. God's prophet who confronted David with his sin was Nathan.
8. The child died.
9. Solomon

Review
1. Saul spared him.
2. He was nine feet tall and a fierce warrior.
3. Saul was his father.
4. A Philistine city
5. He fell on his sword.
6. Saul was jealous and wanted to kill him.
7. See the master list on page 274.

DAVID AND ABSALOM
Worksheet
1. II Samuel 15–19; c. 990 B.C.
2. He had a handsome head of hair. He was David's son.
3. He sat at the gate and gave attention to the people.
4. He fled Jerusalem.
5. Hushai
6. Attack immediately
7. He waited.
8. His hair got caught.
9. While he was caught in the tree, Joab killed him.
10. He was deeply sad.

Test
1. II Samuel 15–19; c. 990 B.C.
2. He had a handsome head of hair. He was David's son.
3. He sat at the gate and gave attention to the people.
4. He fled Jerusalem.
5. Hushai was a follower of David who went with Absalom to give him bad advice.
6. Attack immediately
7. He said to wait to attack and gather all Israel to himself.
8. David said to deal gently with Absalom.

ANSWERS

9. While he was caught in the tree by his hair, Joab killed him.
10. He was deeply sad.

Review
1. A donkey's jawbone
2. The statue of Dagon fell over. It was set back up, but the next day it was lying before the Ark with its head and hands broken off.
3. 40
4. It is a song written by David lamenting the deaths of Saul and Jonathan.
5. His men entered through the water supply.
6. He was struck dead when he touched the Ark trying to steady it.
7. See the master list on page 274.

SOLOMON'S REIGN
Worksheet
1. I Kings 1-11, II Chronicles 1-9; c. 971-931 B.C.
2. David
3. Wisdom
4. During Solomon's reign there was peace in Israel.
5. Answers will vary.
6. The Queen of Sheba
7. Late in life Solomon was tempted by foreign women, and he turned from God.
8. 40 years

Project 1
When David was very old, Adonijah made sacrifice and held a feast claiming to be king. He did not invite Solomon, Nathan, or the others who knew he was not the right king. Nathan told Bathsheba of what Adonijah did, and Bathsheba went to David. David made Solomon king. Adonijah was scared and took hold of the horns of the altar. Solomon spared him.

Project 2 - Proverbs
1. does not overeat
2. does not overstay his welcome
3. honest
4. generous
5. does not vent all his feelings
6. thinks about what he says
7. humble

1. hard working
2. earns money
3. generous/charitable
4. prepared

5. strong, honorable, happy
6. wise
7. praised by others

Test
1. I Kings 1-11, II Chronicles 1-9; c. 971-931 B.C.
2. Wisdom
3. Wealth
4. Solomon built the temple. Answers will vary.
5. To see his temple and wealth
6. Late in life Solomon was tempted by foreign women, and he turned from God.
7. 40 years
8. Rehoboam

Review
1. Answers will vary.
2. Food
3. He would not raise his hand against God's anointed.
4. The King of Tyre
5. David
6. See the master list on page 274.

SOLOMON GIVEN WISDOM
Worksheet
1. I Kings 3; c. 970 B.C.
2. Maturity
3. God appeared to Solomon in his sleep and asked him what his heart desired.
4. He requested wisdom because he knew he was inexperienced and did not know how to rule the nation.
5. Wealth and power
6. To hear his wisdom and be instructed in the Word of God

Project 1
The parties involved: two harlots who both had babies
The problem: One baby died and both women claimed the living child was her son
Solomon's solution: Cut the baby in half and give each mother half
How the parties reacted to Solomon's solution: One woman said to do it, but the other said to let the baby live and go to the other woman.
Solomon's final verdict: Give the baby to the woman who was willing to give it up so that it might live.

ANSWERS

Project 2
1. law
2. life
3. esteem
4. direct
5. overflow
6. my son
wisdom

Test
1. I Kings 3; c. 970 B.C.
2. God appeared to Solomon in his sleep and asked him what his heart desired.
3. He requested wisdom because he knew he was inexperienced and did not know how to rule the nation.
4. Wealth and power
5. Nobility from the ends of the earth came to be instructed in the Word of God.

Review
1. David had him killed.
2. David is known as the most prominent king of Israel.
3. Ish-Bosheth
4. Every six paces
5. Lament
6. See the master list on page 274.

THE WRITINGS OF SOLOMON
Worksheet
1. Proverbs and Ecclesiastes; c. 970 B.C.
2. Peace and prosperity
3. Even more than his father, David, Solomon was a patron of the arts.
4. 3000
5. Ecclesiastes
6. Life apart from God
7. Fear God and keep his commandments

Project 2
RIGHTEOUS
v. 1 makes father happy
v. 4 diligent
v. 5 gathers in summer
v. 16 labor leads to life
v. 20 speaks value
v. 23 has wisdom
v. 25 has an everlasting foundation
v. 27 has prolonged days

WICKED
v. 1 makes father grieve
v. 4 a slacker
v. 5 sleeps in harvest
v. 16 wages lead to sin
v. 20 heart is worthless
v. 23 evil is like a sport
v. 25 is no more
v. 27 short days

Project 3
1. the preacher
2. vanity
3. sun and wind
4. under the sun
5. wisdom, vanity
6. pleasure, vanity
7. wisdom, Wise men die and are forgotten just like foolish men.
8. Work, vanity
9. Food and drink, vanity
10. To be born, die, kill, heal, weep, laugh, dance...
11. Fear God and keep his commandments for God will judge every work.

Test
1. Proverbs and Ecclesiastes; c. 970 B.C.
2. Solomon's reign was marked by peace and prosperity which come from wise rule.
3. Even more than his father, David, Solomon was a patron of the arts.
4. 3000
5. Ecclesiastes is one of the earliest philosophy books in the world.
6. Life apart from God
7. Fear God and keep his commandments

Review
1. By calling to the boy that the arrows were beyond him, Jonathan warned David that he should flee for his life.
2. The mountain on which David built his stronghold
3. Bathsheba's husband, who was killed by David
4. He was tempted by foreign women to follow false gods.
5. Wealth and power
6. See the master list on page 274.

ANSWERS

THE TEMPLE IS BUILT

Worksheet
1. I Kings 6-8; c. 967-960 B.C.
2. Tyre
3. Cedar trees, gold and treasures, skilled metal worker
4. Made the furnishings of the temple
5. The blocks were cut and fitted at the quarry.
6. It was overlaid with gold.
7. The temple was built to be awe-inspiring and beautiful.
8. Pillars, pomegranates, cherubim
9. Seven years
10. The priests could not remain in the building.

Project 1
Building Supplies
stone
cedar boards
cypress planks
gold
olive wood
bronze
Decorations
buds
flowers
overlaid with gold
cherubim
palm trees
lattice network
pomegranates
lilies
lions, oxen, cherubim

Project 2
ornamental buds and open flowers
gold overlay and gold chains
carved figures of cherubim, palm trees and open flowers
two pillars with lily-shaped bronze capitals sporting a lattice network with wreaths of chains and two rows of pomegranates

Test
1. I Kings 6-8; c. 967-960 B.C.
2. Answers will vary. See card.

Review
1. Eli
2. Imprecatory
3. Jebus

4. Their child died.
5. He had a handsome head of hair and was David's son.
6. 40 years
7. See the master list on page 274.

THE QUEEN OF SHEBA VISITS SOLOMON

Worksheet
1. I Kings 10; c. 950 B.C.
2. To test him with difficult questions
3. She had a large entourage that brought gifts including gold and spices.
4. Her expectations were surpassed.
5. The people and officials
6. Gifts of gold and spices

Project 1

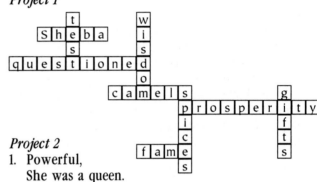

Project 2
1. Powerful, She was a queen.
2. Skeptical, She wanted to test Solomon for herself.
3. Impressed, She saw the great wealth and prosperity of Solomon's kingdom.
4. God-fearing, She acknowledged God as the source of Solomon's prosperity.
5. Generous, She gave Solomon great gifts.

Test
1. I Kings 10; c. 950 B.C.
2. Solomon was known around the world as a just king.
3. To test him with difficult questions
4. She had a large entourage that brought gifts including gold and spices.
5. Her expectations were surpassed.
6. The people and officials
7. Gifts of gold and spices

Review
1. He pushed over the pillars supporting the building, so it collapsed on the crowd of Philistines.
2. Lament, confession, praise, thanksgiving, imprecatory
3. Adultery
4. He got stuck in a tree hanging by his hair. Some of

ANSWERS

David's soldiers spotted him and Joab killed him.
5. Wisdom
6. See the master list on page 274.

THE END OF SOLOMON'S REIGN
Worksheet
1. I Kings 11; c. 931 B.C.
2. He did not follow the Lord whole-heartedly.
3. It would cause their hearts to be led away from the Lord.
4. Places of worship for their pagan gods
5. Enemies
6. His kingdom was broken.

Project 1
1. foreign wives—Solomon had many foreign wives
2. high places—He built high places to the false gods
3. burned incense—At the high places his wives burned incense to their gods
4. turned his heart—Solomon turned his heart from God in his old age
5. tear the kingdom away—God decided to tear the kingdom away from him
6. not obey the Lord—Solomon did not obey the Lord by marrying women who worshiped other gods

Project 2
Solomon got his wisdom by asking for it instead of anything else. An example of his wisdom is that he determined which woman was the mother of the living child.

Solomon had a weakness for women. The result was that they turned from God.

Solomon's work: he built the temole, he wrote Proverbs and Ecclesiastes, and he had a peaceful and prosperous reign over Israel.

Test
1. I Kings 11; c. 931 B.C.
2. He did not obey the Lord.
3. He married foreign women and built places of worship for their pagan gods.
4. It would cause their hearts to be led away from the Lord.
5. God raised up enemies and his kingdom was broken.

Review
1. David's wife who was ashamed of his dancing before the Lord
2. Nathan
3. While he was sleeping, the Lord came to him and asked him what his heart desired. Solomon

requested wisdom.
4. 3000
5. Gold and spices
6. See the master list on page 274.

ISRAEL DIVIDES INTO TWO KINGDOMS
Worksheet
1. I Kings 12, II Chronicles 10; c. 931 B.C.
2. He built places of worship for his wives to worship their pagan gods.
3. His kingdom was taken away from him.
4. For the sake of his father, David
5. Ahijah was the prophet who told Jeroboam that he would rule ten of the tribes of Israel.
6. He increased the burden of their work.
7. Jeroboam

Project 1
1. "Please take away some of the heavy burden Solomon made us carry."
2. "Depart for three days, and then come back."
3. "Be kind to the people and they will be your servants forever."
4. What advice do the young men have?"
5. Make their work harder."
6. "Things will be a lot harder under me than they were under my father."
7. "We will not serve under you."

Project 2
1. He built two calves of gold and set them up in Dan and Bethel.
2. He did not want the people to go to Jerusalem to offer sacrifices and have their hearts turned back to follow Rehoboam.
3. One was in the North and the other was in the South. Everyone was close to one of them.
4. A feast, priests for his high places, and a new calendar

Test
1. I Kings 12, II Chronicles 10; c. 931 B.C.
2. Solomon angered God by building places of worship for his wives to worship their pagan gods.
3. His kingdom would be taken away from him.
4. The punishment would not come in his lifetime.
5. Ahijah was the prophet who told Jeroboam that he would rule ten of the tribes of Israel.
6. Jeroboam was Solomon's servant. Rehoboam was Solomon's son.
7. He increased the burden of their work.
8. Ten

ANSWERS

Review
1. Jonathan was David's close friend as well as Saul's son.
2. She was ashamed of David's humility when he danced before the Lord.
3. He was put on the front line, and then Joab pulled the other men back from him.
4. Wait to attack and gather all of Israel to himself
5. Fear God and keep his commandments
6. See the master list on page 274.

KINGS OF ISRAEL
Worksheet
1. I & II Kings, I & II Chronicles; c. 931-722 B.C.
2. Ten
3. North
4. They did not conquer all of the Canaanites. They were quickly corrupted by the pagans.
5. Jeroboam
6. There were no righteous kings.
7. Payment to another nation
8. Assyria
9. There was political turmoil and spiritual decay. The reigns of the final kings were short. The kingdom was split, as more than one man claimed to be king.

Project 1
1. Zimri
2. Elah
3. Omri
4. Zimri
5. Baasha
6. Omri
7. Baasha
8. Omri
9. in the way of Jeroboam

Project 2
Israel

Jeroboam	22	-
Nadab	2	-
Baasha	24	-
Elah	2	-
Zimri	7 days	-
Omri	12	-
Ahab	22	-
Ahaziah	2	-
Joram	12	-
Jehu	28	
Jehoahaz	17	-
Jehoash	16	-
Jeroboam II	41	-
Zechariah	6 mo.	-
Shallum	1 mo	
Menahem	10	-
Pakahiah	2	-
Pekah	20	-
Hoshea	9	-

Test
1. I & II Kings, I & II Chronicles; c. 931-722 B.C.
2. The kings of Israel ruled ten tribes in the northern region of the old unified Israel.
3. They were not faithful to conquer all of the Canaanites.
4. Jeroboam was divided Israel's first king. He was Solomon's servant.
5. He was the last king.
6. Assyria
7. The reigns of the final kings were short in length, and more than one man claimed to be king.

Review
1. Othniel—the first judge; Samuel—the last judge; Gideon—sent away soldiers that knelt to drink; Deborah—a woman judge; Gideon—asked God to make fleece wet and the ground dry; Jephthah—vowed to sacrifice the first thing that came out of his house
2. The inside was overlaid with gold. It was decorated with pillars, pomegranates, and cherubim.
3. See the master list on page 274.

KINGS OF JUDAH
Worksheet
1. I & II Kings, I & II Chronicles; c. 931-586 B.C.
2. Rehoboam
3. He made their work harder.
4. He was Solomon's son.
5. Judah and Benjamin
6. Some of the Israelites living near Judah joined the Southern Kingdom because they saw God's presence with Judah.
7. Judah had several righteous kings.
8. God was gracious on Judah to grant longer reigns to the righteous kings.
9. Babylon

Project 1
Asa
Good
1. Removed altars to foreign gods

ANSWERS

2. Fortified cities
3. Removed Maachah from being queen mother

Bad
1. Did not remove all of the high places
2. Made a treaty with Syria

Azariah (also called Uzziah)

Good
1. Defeated the Philistines
2. Strengthened the army and cities

Bad
1. He burned incense on the altar
2. He got angry with the priests

Project 2
Judah

Rehoboam	17	-
Abijami	3	-
Asa	41	+
Jehoshaphat	25	+
Jehoram	8	-
Ahaziah	1	-
Athaliah	6	-
Joash	40	+
Amaziah	29	+
Azariah	52	+
Jotham	16	+
Ahaz	16	-
Hezekiah	29	+
Manasseh	55	-
Amon	2	-
Josiah	31	+
Jehoahaz	3 mo	-
Jehoiakim	11	-
Jehoiachin	3 mo	-
Zedekiah	11	-

Test
1. I & II Kings, I & II Chronicles; c. 931–586 B.C.
2. Rehoboam was Solomon's son. He made their work harder.
3. Two, Judah and Benjamin
4. Some of the Israelites living near Judah joined the Southern Kingdom because they saw God's presence with Judah.
5. Judah had several righteous kings.
6. God was gracious to Judah to grant longer reigns to the righteous kings.
7. Babylon

Review
1. David committed adultery; Saul was hiding in the baggage; Solomon built the temple; David captured Mt. Zion; David brought the Ark back to Jerusalem;

Saul disobeyed God by not killing all the animals of the enemy; Solomon—many nobles visited him
2. Absalom
3. See the master list on this page.

JUDGES-KINGS BIBLE CARDS *Master List*

The Judges | c. 1389–1050 B.C.
Othniel and Ehud | *Judges 3* | c. 1377–1337 B.C.
Deborah the Prophetess | *Judges 4, 5* | c. 1350 B.C.
Gideon Delivers Israel | *Judges 6, 7* | c. 1350 B.C.
Jephthah's Foolish Vow | *Judges 11, 12* | c. 1350 B.C.
Naomi and Ruth | *Ruth 1–4* | c. 1100 B.C.
Samson and Delilah | *Judges 13–16* | c. 1080 B.C.
Hannah and Eli | *I Samuel 1–2* | c. 1075 B.C.
Samuel, The Last Judge of Israel | *I Samuel 2–4* | c. 1065 B.C.
The Ark Is Taken Into Captivity | *I Samuel 4–6* | c. 1050 B.C.
Saul, the First King of Israel | *I Samuel 9, 10* | c. 1043 B.C.
The Genealogy of David | *I Chronicles 2* | c. 1041 B.C.
Saul's Sin at Amalek | *I Samuel 15* | c. 1032 B.C.
David is Anointed as King | *I Samuel 16* | c. 1030 B.C.
David and Goliath | *I Samuel 17* | c. 1028 B.C.
Jonathan Protects David | *I Samuel 20* | c. 1020 B.C.
The Deaths of Saul and Jonathan | *I Samuel 31* | c. 1011 B.C.
Davidic Kingdom | *I & II Samuel, I Chronicles* | c. 1011–971 B.C.
The Conquest of Jerusalem | *II Samuel 5* | c. 1003 B.C.
The Ark Enthroned in Jerusalem | *II Samuel 6* | c. 1000 B.C.
David Writes Many Psalms | *Psalms* | c. 1000 B.C.
David and Bathsheba | *II Samuel 11–12* | c. 995 B.C.
David and Absalom | *II Samuel 15–19* | c. 990 B.C.
Solomon's Reign | *I Kings 1–11, II Chronicles 1–9* | c. 971–931 B.C.
Solomon Given Wisdom | *I Kings 3* | c. 970 B.C.
The Writings of Solomon | *Proverbs and Ecclesiastes* | c. 970 B.C.
The Temple is Built | *I Kings 6–8* | c. 967–960 B.C.
The Queen of Sheba Visits Solomon | *I Kings 10* | c. 950 B.C.
The End of Solomon's Reign | *I Kings 11* | c. 931 B.C.
Israel Divides Into Two Kingdoms | *I Kings 12, II Chronicles 10* | c. 931 B.C.
Kings of Israel | *I & II Kings, I & II Chronicles* | c. 931–722 B.C.
Kings of Judah | *I & II Kings, I & II Chronicles* | c. 931–586 B.C.

Project 2—Poster

Make a poster showing the cycle of events that happened over and over again in the book of Judges. Make bubbles like the bubbles below. Fill in the blanks in the information on the bubbles. Place the first event at the top middle. Arrange the bubbles in a clockwise circle in chronological order. Glue all the bubbles in place. With crayons or markers draw arrows between the bubbles showing the clockwise direction in which the bubbles are to be read. Around the circle you may illustrate what is described in the bubbles.

The Judges

The Israelites
go after
_____
and forsake
_____ .

God
raises
up a
_____ .

The Israelites
cry out to
_____ .

The
Israelites
are _____ .

God punishes
Israel by allowing
_____
to _____
_____ them.

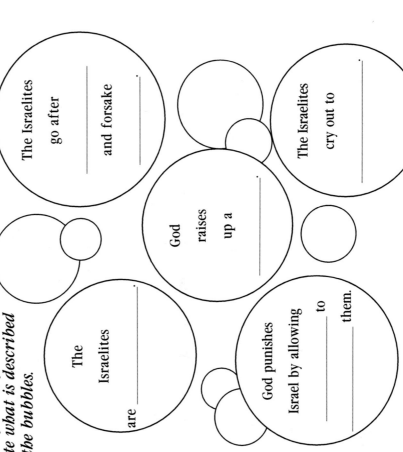

Worksheet

1. What is the date for the Judges?

2. List two specific sins of the Israelites in the time of the judges.

3. What does God do to punish the Israelites when they sin?

4. What does God do when the people cry out to him?

5. Who determined who would be the judge?

6. Name three major judges.

Project 1—Bible Reading

Read Judges 1. Unscramble the words below and write them in the correct blank.

dedi
boajus
notnais
ddeerlunp
meniees
gujesd
alabs

1. Israel served the Lord until _____ died.

2. The Israelites forsook the Lord and instead served the _____.

3. God handed Israel over to their _____.

4. Israel was oppressed and _____.

5. God raised up _____ to deliver them.

6. When the judge _____ the people became corrupt again.

7. God no longer drove out the _____ which remained in the land when Joshua died.

Othniel and Ehud

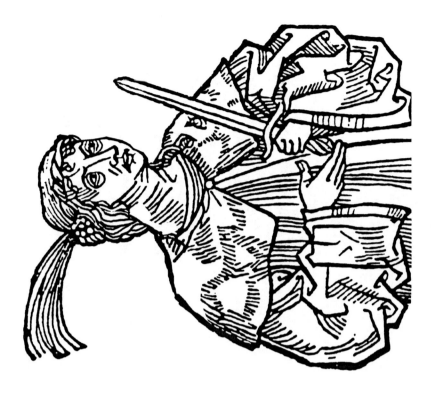

Project 2—Covert Judge Poster

In Judges 3:12-30 we learn of the daring escapades of "Ehud, the Left-Handed Agent of God." Create your own movie poster advertizing a movie about Ehud's action-packed adventure, or title and color in the poster begun below. Include the exotic location of the story and the very fat foe.

From BENJAMIN, *the Tribe of* BENJAMIN:

EHUD

Worksheet

1. What is the Scripture reference and date for Othniel and Ehud?

2. What king did God allow to oppress Israel because they sinned? (during Othniel's life)

3. Who was Othniel?

4. Who was Eglon?

5. Describe how Eglon was killed.

6. What happened after Eglon was killed?

Project 1—Bible Reading

Read in Judges 3 about Othniel and Ehud. As you read each story you should be able to identify each part of the cycle of Judges. Write the verse in which you find each part of the cycle in the space below.

Othniel

Israel worships other gods.

God hands Israel over to its enemies.

Israel cries out to God.

God sends a judge._____

Israel is freed.
_____

Ehud

Israel worships other gods._____

God hands Israel over to its enemies._____

Israel cries out to God._____

God sends a judge._____

Israel is freed._____

Project 2

When Israel routed Jabin's army, his commander, Sisera, fled on foot to Jael's tent. Label this picture of Jael's tent.

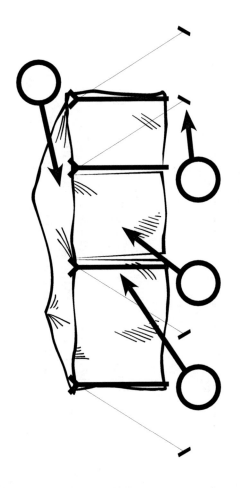

1. TENT DOOR: a flap of cloth that could be raised and lowered. The only man allowed inside a tent was the father of the family.
2. TENT POLES: wooden poles that were stuck in the ground
3. COVERINGS: cloth or goats' hair that was stretched over the tent poles and tied down with cords. The coverings would shrink after rain fell on it so that it was then waterproof.
4. TENT PEGS: wooden pegs which pulled tight the cords and coverings. The pegs were hammered into the ground.

Deborah, the Prophetess

Worksheet

1. What is the Scripture reference and date for Deborah the Prophetess?

2. In addition to being a judge, what other job did Deborah have?

3. Who was Sisera?

4. Whom did Deborah summon to lead Israel in battle? What response did she get?

5. What was the consequence of Barak's hesitance?

6. To whose tent did Sisera flee?

7. What did she do to Sisera?

Project 1–Bible Reading

Read Judges 4, 5 about Deborah's time as a judge. Then put the adjectives or descriptive phrases below under the name of the person that they describe.

Received a drink from his killer | sat under a palm tree | killed Sisera | had 900 chariots of iron | commander of the enemy army | commander of the Israelite army | prophetess | called the enemy to her tent | would not go by himself | judge | King of Canaan | ran away on foot |

Deborah

_____

_____

Barak

_____

_____

Jabin

_____

_____

Jael

_____

_____

Sisera

_____

_____

Project 2

Glue a photocopy of "Gideon"
written backwards to the wrong
side of a 4"x11" piece of fleece.
Cut out the backward letters
and fleece. On another sheet
of paper, glue the letters with
the fleece side up to spell Gideon.
The background may be decorated to look
like ground. Draw a line between the d and the e.
Use blue construction paper to cut out many water droplets. On the left half of the paper glue water droplets to
the fleece but not the ground. On the right half glue water
droplets to the ground but not the fleece.

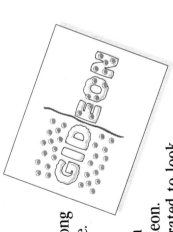

Gideon Delivers
Israel

Worksheet

1. What is the Scripture reference and date for Gideon Delivers Israel?

2. What sign did Gideon ask of God before he went into battle with the Midianites?

3. What two groups of people did Gideon send away from the army?

4. Why did God have Gideon reduce the number of men that would go into battle?

5. With how many men did Gideon go into battle?

6. At what time of day did Gideon and his men attack the Midianites?

7. How did the Israelites defeat the Midianites?

Project 1–Bible Reading

Read about Gideon in Judges 6:28–7:3. Then fill in the spaces in the outline below.

I. GIDEON LEADS SPIRITUALLY.

A. Gideon's _____ built an altar to ___ and an Asherah that the people _____.

  1. God told Gideon to _____.

  2. Gideon goes _____ because he is afraid of _____.

B. The people find the atlar and the Asherah _____.

  1. They found out that Gideon destroyed them and wanted to _____.

  2. Gideon's _____ said to let Baal _____.

II. GIDEON LEADS MILITARILY.

A. Gideon asks for a _____.

  1. Gideon says if the fleece is _____ and the ground is _____ in the morning he will know that God _____.

  2. In the morning the _____ is _____ and the _____ is _____. Gideon then asks that the next morning the _____ be _____ and the _____ be _____. God _____ this sign.

B. Gideon chooses his men.

Project 2—Timbrel

Jephthah vowed that if God would grant Israel military success, he would sacrifice the first living thing that he saw come out of his house. When he returned home victorious, his daughter came out to greet him playing the timbrel. The timbrel is a musical instrument made of a wooden hoop with animal hides stretched over the top and bottom. It is played by hitting the stretched hides with one hand while holding it in the other hand. Have students make a small model of a timbrel. You will need a round oatmeal box, sheet of cardboard, paint, and hot glue. Cut the top of the oatmeal box leaving about a two inch band attached to the top. Lay the top on the cardboard sheet and trace around the edge. Cut the cardboard sheet about 1/2 inch larger than the tracing. Hot glue the cardboard circle to the band of the oatmeal box. Allow the glue to dry before painting or decorating your timbrel.

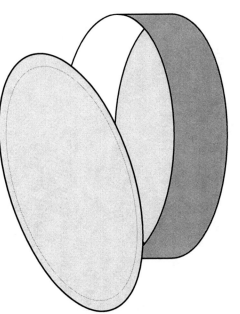

Jephthah's Foolish Vow

Worksheet

1. What is the Scripture reference and date for Jephthah's Foolish Vow?

2. From what nation did God raise up Jephthah to deliver the Gileadites?

3. Why were the Ephraimites angry with the Gileadites?

4. Who won the battle between the Gileadites and the Ephraimites?

5. How did Jephthah and the Gileadites determine who the Ephraimite survivors were?

6. What had Jephthah vowed to God?

7. What happened when Jephthah returned from battle victorious?

8. What happened to Jepthah's line because of his vow?

Project 1—Bible Reading

Read about Jephthah in Judges 11. Then fill in the spaces in the outline below.

I. Jephthah's background

A. He was a Gileadite. His father was _____.

B. His mother was a _____.

C. His brothers chased him _____.

II. Jephthah delivers Israel.

A. Jephthah sends _____ to the king of the _____ asking him to give back the _____ he had taken from _____.

B. Jephthah _____ king would not listen to Jephthah. The _____ to God that if God gave him the victory, he would _____ whatever first came _____.

C. God gives Israel _____.

D. Jephthah's _____ comes out to meet him when he returns victorious.

1. She told him to do to her as he had vowed to God.

2. She requested to hav _____ to _____ with her _____ because she would never _____.

Naomi and Ruth

Project 1—Bible Reading *[continued]*

   2. He had his workers purposely leave behind
_____ for her to get.

B. _____ _____ tells Ruth to lie down at
_____ _____.

C. Boaz will redeem Ruth.

   1. When a husband died and their was no son to carry
on the line, the closest relative would marry the
widow to produce a son to carry on the line.

   2. There was another closer _____ than
Boaz who had the first option of _____ Ruth.

   3. Boaz went to the other _____ and in
front of _____ he gave that man the
choice of buying the _____ from _____
_____ and marrying _____ .

   4. The closer relative did not want to do this, so Boaz
did. Boaz removed his _____ and
_____ it to the other man to show that the
matter was _____ .

   5. _____ married Ruth and they had a
_____ _____.

D. The son of _____ and _____
was named _____. He was the _____
_____ of David.

Worksheet

1. What is the Scripture reference and date for Naomi and Ruth?

2. How was Ruth related to Naomi?

3. Where did Naomi and Ruth go after the men in the family died?

4. What does the name Mara mean?

5. Who left grain for Ruth so that she and Naomi could survive?

6. What did Ruth do to make Boaz decide that he wanted to marry her?

7. Whom did Boaz have to talk to before he could possibly marry Ruth?

8. How were Ruth and Boaz related to King David? Who is the most famous person that descended from Ruth?

9. What does a kinsman-redeemer do?

Project 1–Bible Reading

Read about Naomi and Ruth in Ruth 1–4. Then fill in the spaces in the outline below.

I. The characters
A. Naomi: an Israelite woman who went to _____ with her two _____. Her sons married Naomi's _____ women, and then both sons and Naomi's _____ died.
B. Ruth: a _____ woman who married one of _____ sons. She left her parents and home to stay with _____.
C. Boaz: a close _____ of Naomi

II. The problem
A. Naomi lost both sons and her husband. She was in a _____ country.
B. There was a famine so Naomi returned to _____ where she hoped she could find _____. In Israel you were only allowed to pick your field once. Anything that was missed was to be available to the poor and widows. Naomi sent _____ to search for grain after the pickers.

III. The solution
A. Boaz saw _____ in his fields and commanded his workers to help her.
1. He let her _____ and _____ with his workers.

Samson and Delilah

Project 2—Biblical Art Study

Discuss Rembrandt's The Blinding of Samson.

1. Who are the soldiers in the painting?

2. What appears to be the job of the man in the foreground holding the halberd (ax-like blade on a long shaft)? What is his "job" as part of the painting?

3. As Delilah rushes out of the tent, what emotions does she seem to be experiencing?

4. What things are out of place in the painting if the work is showing an event from the time of the Judges?

Worksheet

1. What is the Scripture reference and date for Samson and Delilah?

2. From what nation did God deliver Israel by raising up Samson?

3. How was Samson's birth special?

4. Name two things that a Nazarite was not allowed to do.

5. What unusual "weapon" did Samson use to kill a thousand Philistines?

6. With what Philistine woman did Samson fall in love?

7. What was the secret of Samson's great strength?

8. Describe how the Philistines finally captured Samson and tell what they did to him?

9. Describe Samson's death.

Project 1—Bible Reading

There are several interesting stories from the life of Samson. Students are to read one or more of these stories in the passages suggested below. Then write a paragraph on each story read which explains what happened, including at least five details or facts not listed on the card. For teachers with multiple students it is suggested that the stories be divided among the students. When each student has completed his assignment, they can take turns reading their paragraphs to others.

Story Passages

Samson's Birth (Judges 13)
Samson and the Riddle (Judges 14)
Samson Kills Many Philistines (Judges 15)
Samson and Delilah (Judges 16:1-22)
Samson's Death (Judges 16:23-31)

Hannah and Eli

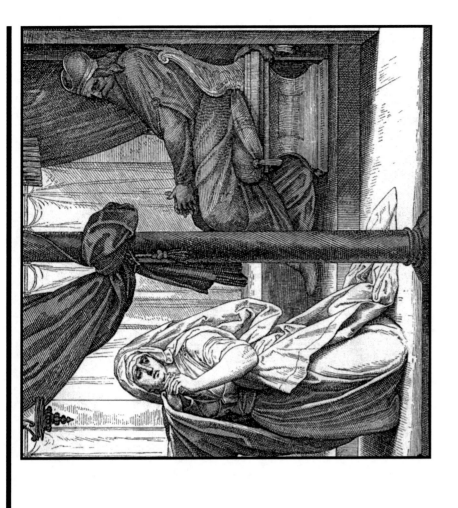

Project 2–Clothespin Figures

MATERIALS
3 wooden clothespins
felt/fabric
pipe cleaners
small wiggly eyes
yarn/string
fine tip pen
glue

Make clothespin figures of Hannah, Eli, Peninnah, and Baby Samuel to act out this story. Wrap the center of 4" pipe cleaner around the "neck" of each clothespin once. Twist and bend the two ends of the pipe cleaner to make arms. Trim the ends to adjust the length if needed. Glue wiggly eyes to the "head" of each clothespin and glue yarn to make hair. Using a fine tip pen draw other facial features as desired. Cut clothes from the felt or fabric and glue them to the clothespins. Make a small bundle of cloth to be a swaddled baby Samuel. Cut a small circle of paper and draw a face on it. Glue this face of the end of the bundle of cloth. Now you have characters to act out the story of Hannah and Eli.

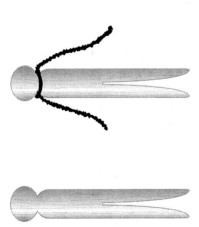

Worksheet

1. What is the Scripture reference and date for Hannah and Eli?

2. Why did Elkanah and his wives go up to Shiloh?

3. What was Hannah's problem? Who harassed her about the problem?

4. What wouldn't Hannah do because she was so upset by her problem? What did she do instead?

5. Who was Eli?

6. What vow did Hannah make?

7. What did Eli think was wrong with Hannah?

8. What was the name of the child born to Hannah?

9. When did Hannah fulfill her vow?

Project 1–Bible Reading

Read in I Samuel 1-2 about Hannah and Eli. Then complete the word find below and be sure to know what each word has to do with the story.

```
H A N N A A H E L K A N N A H V
E O W E A N E D N E D B U S T A
P V R D A L P H P S W O R D E L
T W A D H R A Z E R W E A N E O
W E A N E A C H I L O L E S S U
T S D R O N N R T Y U V O W I C
E A S E L I C N V B N M O P O H
L M B S L S C X A Z C V K N I
K U V E S K V B N H G H J K E L
A E V P R S A W E R L G W D A D
N L E R A N S N S U K R O R M L
A P R E Z L A S A T J A R U O E
S A I S O E M C S H H C K N E S
D O T S R S A K L S Y E S K L S
G L A G U L F J W E P T F G H J
H N S H Y I G H G H B I B L E A B C
```

Hannah	tabernacle	Eli
Elkanah	wept	drunk
provoked	vow	Samuel
childless	razor	weaned

Samuel, the Last Judge of Israel

Project 1–Bible Reading *[continued]*

Using the graph on the preceeding page, on another sheet of paper, answer the questions below.

1. What do you notice about the length of their enslavement as the cycle of faithlessness, repentance, and deliverance repeated time and time again?

2. What do you notice about the length of their freedom as the cycle was repeated over and over again?

3. What do you notice about the difference between the lengths of their enslavement and freedom as the cycle is repeated over time?

Worksheet

1. What is the Scripture reference and date for Samuel, the Last Judge of Israel?

2. How had Hophni and Phinehas sinned?

3. Describe how God called Samuel.

4. What was the message that God gave to Samuel about Eli's family?

5. Samuel saw the rise and fall of _____ and he anointed _____ as king of Israel.

Project 1—Bible Reading

Make a chart and/or bar graph showing the length of time in which the people were enslaved and freed during the time of some of the judges. Fill in the chart below first. Each box has the Scripture reference for where to find the information.

Years of Enslavement and Freedom During the Judges

Judge	Enslavement		Freedom	
Othniel	Judges 3:8 [ ] years		Judges 3:11 [ ] years	
Ehud	Judges 3:14 [ ] years		Judges 3:30 [ ] years	
Deborah	Judges 4:3 [ ] years		Judges 5:31 [ ] years	
Gideon	Judges 6:1 [ ] years		Judges 8:28 [ ] years	
Jephthah	Judges 10:8 [ ] years		Judges 12:7 [ ] years	
Samson	Judges 13:1 [ ] years		Judges 15:20 [ ] years	

Project 1—Bible Reading [continued]

Now use the same information to complete the bar graph. The bars of Othniel are drawn for you. Color all the bars showing years of enslavement in one color. Color all the bars showing years of freedom in a different color.

Years of Enslavement and Freedom During the Judges

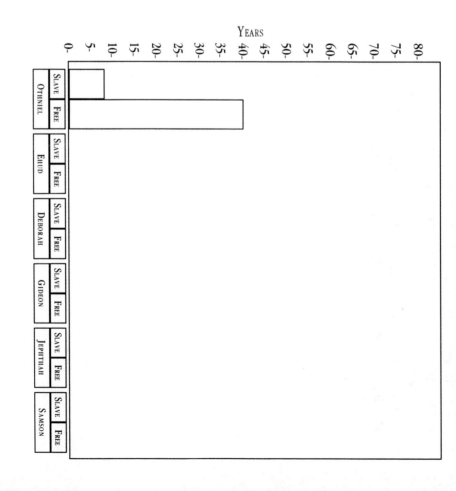

Project 2

Strange things have been happening to the Philistines ever since they captured Israel's Ark of the Covenant. On another piece of paper, write a letter to the editor of the Philistine Gazette voicing your desire (you are to write as a Philistine) to send the Ark back. Be sure to describe the trouble caused by the Ark.

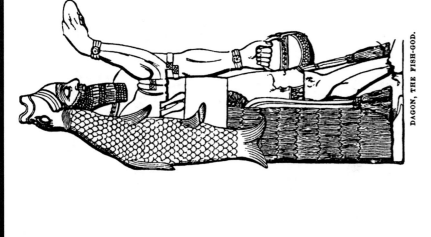

DAGON, THE FISH-GOD.

The Ark is Taken into Captivity

Worksheet

1. What is the Scripture reference and date for the Ark is Taken Into Captivity?

2. Why did the Israelites take the Ark into battle?

3. Name two results of the battle on the day that the ark was taken along.

4. How did Eli die?

5. Who captured the Ark?

6. Where did they keep the Ark at first? What happened while the Ark was there?

7. What happened in the cities where the Ark was kept?

8. Describe how they sent the Ark back to Israel.

Project 1—Bible Reading

Read in I Samuel 4–6 about the Ark being taken into captivity. Look at the phrases and sentence below. Decide which part of speech each word is and then write it under the proper heading.

PHILISTINES CAPTURED THE ARK

WICKED HOPHNI DIED.

DAGON FELL BACKWARDS.

FIVE GOLDEN TUMORS

FINALLY HITCHED A CART

TWO MILK COWS

Nouns

_____

_____

_____

Verbs

_____

_____

_____

Adjectives

_____

_____

_____

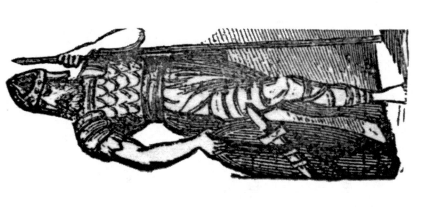

Saul, the First King of Israel

Review

1. What did God do for his people when they cried out to

    him because of the oppression they were suffering?

2. How was Naomi related to Ruth?

3. How was Samson's birth special?

4. How did Samson die?

5. Who harassed Hannah about her problem?

6. What was the message that God gave to Samuel

    about Eli's family?

Worksheet

1. What is the Scripture reference and date for Saul, the First King of Israel?

2. Who was anointed as judges when Samuel grew old?

3. What kind of people were the new judges? Include one point of proof.

4. How did the people react to the new judges?

5. About what did God have Samuel warn the people?

6. Who was Israel's first king?

7. Why did Saul go to Samuel?

8. Describe how Samuel announced to the people who would be king.

9. Where was Saul when the announcement was made to the people?

Project 1—Bible Reading

Read about Saul being anointed as the first king of Israel in I Samuel 9, 10. Then complete the following statements. Use the number of blanks and letter clues to help you.

1. Saul was from the tribe of _ e _ _ _ _ _.

2. Saul was a _ _ _ _ s _ _ _ man.

3. Saul was looking for his _ _ _ t _ _ _' donkeys.

4. He only had one-fourth of a _ _ _ _ _ _ l of silver to pay Samuel.

5. Saul found Samuel on his way to make a s _ _ _ _ _ _ _ at a h _ _ h _ _ _ _.

6. Samuel took a _ l _ _ _ of oil and anointed Saul.

7. Saul met a group of p _ _ p _ _ _ and God enabled him to prophesy.

8. When Saul was announced as king he was hiding behind the _ _ _ _ _ _ _.

9. Samuel wrote a book explaining the behavior of _ _ y _ _ _ y.

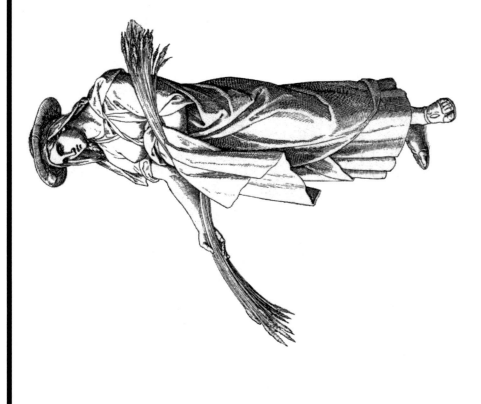

The Genealogy of David

Project 2—Coat of Arms

It was an ancient practice to have a special banner or standard to represent a nation, tribe, or family. A coat of arms is a similar combination of symbols and patterns to represent who a person is and who his ancestors were. Each generation the coat of arms would change, adding in new symbols, some depicting symbols for a child's father and mother's ancestors. *Design a coat of arms for David using at least three symbols or objects which relate to his ancestors. Use your Bible and other resources to recall events from the lives of these ancestors which might give you ideas for symbols.*

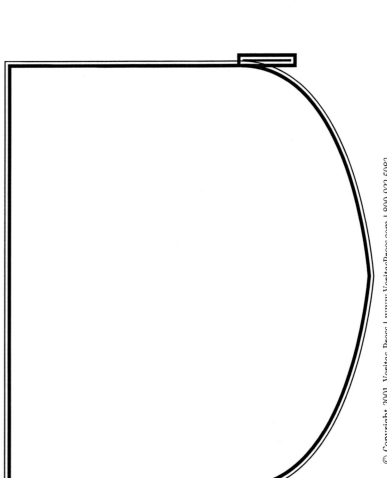

Worksheet

1. What is the Scripture reference and date for the Genealogy of David?

2. Fill in the blanks: _____ , _____ , _____ ,
   Perez, Hezron, Ram, Amminadab,
   Nahshon, Salmon, _____ , _____ , _____ ,
   _____ .

3. Who was the father of Israel?

4. How was Isaac's birth special?

5. What was God showing about himself with Isaac's special birth?

6. What did Jacob's sons become?

7. What was the reputation of the tribe of Judah?

8. Who married Ruth?

9. Who was the son of Ruth?

10. How many sons did Jesse have?

11. Who was Jesse's youngest son?

Project 1—Bible Reading

Read David's genealogy in I Chronicles 2. Then fill in the tree showing Judah's descendants. The first letter of each name is given to help you.

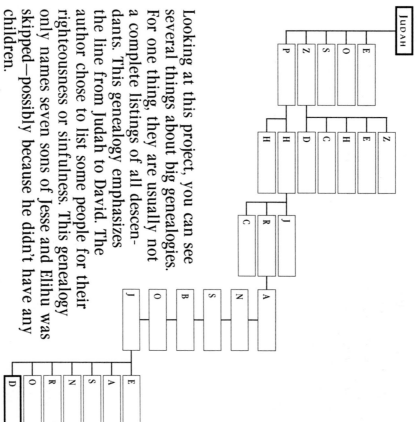

Looking at this project, you can see several things about big genealogies. For one thing, they are usually not a complete listings of all descendants. This genealogy emphasizes the line from Judah to David. The author chose to list some people for their righteousness or sinfulness. This genealogy only names seven sons of Jesse and Elihu was skipped—possibly because he didn't have any children.

If you read the genealogy in Matthew 1, you will see that line has a different emphasis and omits/includes different people.

Saul's Sin at Amalek

Project 2—Comic Strip

Draw a comic strip illustrating this story. Your comic strip must contain at least four scenes. Use dialog bubbles to include important things that were said.

Worksheet

1. What is the Scripture reference and date for Saul's Sin at Amalek?

2. God commanded Saul to kill every _____ and every _____ of the Amalekites.

3. Name two ways in which Saul did not follow the Lord's command.

4. How did Saul greet Samuel after the battle with the Amalekites?

5. Whom did Saul blame for the disobedience concerning the animals?

6. What did Saul say they intended to do with the animals?

7. Who was Agag?

8. What was the punishment for Saul's sin at Amalek?

9. Saul had previously sinned by not waiting for Samuel to _____.

Project 1—Bible Reading

Read in I Samuel 15 about Saul's sin at Amalek. Then fill in the text and crossword puzzle below.

God commanded Saul to (1 down) all of the (2 across). But Saul (3 across) King (2 down) and the best of the cattle and (4 down). The prophet (5 down) was sent by God, and he asked Saul about the (6 across) that was kept by the Israelites. Saul (7 across) the people and said they were going to (8 across) the animals. Because Saul (1 across) God's command he was (9 down) as king. Samuel (10 down) King Agag to pieces.

Project 2—David the Shepherd

*Read over the statements then read David's Psalm 23.
If you see a connection between a verse in the Psalm and
one of the statements about a shepherd, write the verse
number in the blank next to the statement. Not every
statement has a connection to a verse in Psalm 23.*

1. Shepherds carried a club or rod, a sling, and a staff to defend the sheep from wild animals. _____

2. The sheep knew the voice of their shepherd. _____

3. In the summer, the grass near the village dried up, so the shepherd had to take his flock away to find pasture. _____

4. A shepherd's staff was helpful to him when walking in rough country.

5. A shepherd tended sheep and goats in the same flock.

6. A shepherd had to find a good water supply for his flock. _____

7. At night sheep were kept in a sheepfold or cave.

8. A good shepherd leads his sheep; he does not drive them. They will follow him as he walks.

9. A shepherd sometimes watched after all of the sheep in the village. _____

10. Sheep are helpless animals. The shepherd had to provide for their every need. _____

11. A shepherd carried his food in a leather bag called a scrip. _____

David is Anointed as King

Worksheet

1. What is the Scripture reference and date for David is Anointed as King?

2. What information does God give Samuel about the person that will be king?

3. What does Samuel do in order to keep Saul from becoming angry at him?

4. Why does Samuel think that Eliab will be the new king?

5. When Samuel sees the seven sons of Jesse, what question does he ask?

6. Where was Jesse's youngest son?

7. Name two things that God does to Saul after he anoints David.

8. What do his servants suggest to Saul to help with his problem?

9. Who was chosen to serve Saul in this way?

10. What special honor does Saul give to David?

Project 1—Bible Reading

Read about David's anointing as the next king in I Samuel 16. Unscramble the words from the story on the left. Each word matches a phrase on the right so if you get stuck on a scrambled word try to come up with possible words that fit the phrases below. Draw a line connecting each scrambled word with its matching phrase.

FEIRHE   1. tending _____

PRAH   2. the spirit would _____

NORH   3. a _____ to sacrifice

RABERMOAARER   4. looks at the _____

HATER   5. _____ player

TRAPED   6. _____ spirit

EPESH   7. _____ with oil

NITERDSSSIG   8. became his _____

Project 2—Biblical Art Study

Discuss Caravaggio's David with the Head of Goliath.

1. Does this painting show that David killed Goliath at night?

2. How does Caravaggio show who is the morally superior character in the painting?

3. Comparing this painting and the one on the flashcard with the Scripture (1 Sam. 16:18), which shows David's age more accurately?

David and Golith

Worksheet

1. What is the Scripture reference and date for David and Goliath?

2. What was the challenge that Goliath made?

3. How many days did Goliath come forward to make his challenge?

4. From what country was Goliath?

5. Who finally accepted Goliath's challenge?

6. Why was David angry at Goliath?

7. What did Saul give David?

8. How useful was Saul's gift?

9. What weapons did David use to kill Goliath?

Project 1—Bible Reading

Read in I Samuel 17 about David and Goliath. Then write a sentence using the following phrases as they are used in the story.

1. 5,000 shekels

2. one champion

3. forty days

4. three sons

5. ten cheeses

6. five stones

7. no sword

Jonathan Protects David

Project 2—Missing Person Poster

David was on the run, and Saul was after him. Make a wanted poster which might include the following information: Name of person, artist's sketch, physical description, who wants him, and description of any reward offered.

•WANTED•
BY THE KING

Worksheet

1. What is the Scripture reference and date for Jonathan Protects David?

2. Why did David become so popular?

3. Why did Saul want to kill David?

4. How was Jonathan related to Saul?

5. Describe the relationship between Jonathan and David.

6. Why was it necessary to come up with the plan?

7. During what festival did Jonathan carry out his plan to inform David of Saul's intentions?

8. Describe the plan that Jonathan and David had.

9. When the plan was carried out, what did David know he should do?

Project 1—Bible Reading

Read I Samuel 20. Then illustrate the two scenes described below. Use conversation bubbles to include the important things that were said.

JONATHAN LEARNS THAT SAUL IS INDEED PLANNING TO KILL DAVID.

JONATHAN DISCREETLY WARNS DAVID THAT HE IS IN DANGER.

The Deaths of Saul and Jonathan

Project 2—Philistine Headdress

Saul and Jonathan were both killed in a battle against the Philistines. The Philistines had long been in conflict with the Israelites. In battle it would have been easy to determine which were the Philistine enemy by the unique headdresses that they wore. Make a headdress like those worn by the Philistines following the directions below.

Cut a strip of oaktag 1 1/2" wide and about one inch longer than the circumference of the student's head. Place the strip around the student's head to form a band. Hold the overlap on the band and remove the band. Staple the ends of the band where they overlap. Cut a second strip one inch wide and twenty inches long. Staple one end of the strip to the headband. Put the headband back on the student's head with the attached strip right in front of one ear. Pull the strip under the student's jaw and up to reach the top of the headband. Trim the strip to that length to make a chin strap. Punch a hole in the end of the loose chinstrap. With a pencil, put a small mark through the hole on the headband. Remove the headband and place a metal brad through the mark on the headband. Now the headband can be placed on the student's head and the chinstrap can be pulled under his chin and hooked on the metal brad. With spray paint and markers the headdress can be decorated. Glue feathers close together with the quills to the headband all the way around the headband (diagram is incomplete). You may wish to attach another strip of oaktag on the inside of the quills. This "inner headband" will provide more support, durability, and comfort.

Worksheet

1. What is the Scripture reference and date for the Deaths of Saul and Jonathan?

2. Why wouldn't David kill Saul, even though Saul was trying to kill him?

3. Where was David living while it was unsafe for him in Israel?

4. How was Saul wounded?

5. What did Saul ask of his armor-bearer?

6. How did Saul die?

7. Who else died with Saul in the battle?

8. What happened to the soldier who claimed to have killed Saul?

9. What was the song written by David to mourn the deaths of Saul and Jonathan?

Project 1—Bible Reading

Despite the fact that Saul was trying to kill him (and David knew that God had chosen him to be king), David honored Saul and dealt with him righteously. Read I Samuel 26, 31, and II Samuel 1. Then write at least two sentences describing each of three ways in which David was loyal and honoring to a king that had tried to kill him.

1. _____

_____

2. _____

_____

3. _____

_____

Project 2

David's (and his son Solomon's) reign over Israel is considered the height of the kingdom. During this time, the kingdom was expanded to cover the most territory. They enjoyed military dominance (This led to a time of peace during Solomon's reign because no one wanted to challenge them.) There was great wealth and development. David established Jerusalem as his capitol and Solomon built the temple. And the kingdom prospered under the rule of godly and wise kings. Draw a picture depicting one of the kingdoms during this time.

David Kingdom

Worksheet

1. What is the Scripture reference and date for the Davidic Kingdom?

2. From what town was David?

3. What great military feat gave David favor in the eyes of the army and Saul?

4. Why did Saul become jealous of David?

5. What did David have to do since Saul was trying to kill him?

6. About how long did David reign?

7. David was the _____ and most _____ king of Israel

Project 1–Bible Reading

Have the students read one or more stories about David's rule from the passages suggested below. Then write a paragraph on each story read about what happened. For teachers with multiple students it is suggested that the stories be divided among the students. When each student has completed his assignment, they can take turns reading their paragraphs to the others.

STORY PASSAGES

Civil War with Ishbosheth (II Samuel 2)
God's Covenant with David (II Samuel 7)
David's Kindness to Mephibosheth (II Samuel 9)
David takes a Census (II Samuel 24)

The Conquest of Jerusalem

Project 2—Zion

In II Samuel 5:7 Zion is referred to for the first time in the Bible. Originally, "Zion" was the name of a fortified mound. Eventually it came to refer to the whole city of Jerusalem and after that, the entire nation of Israel. Read the following verses and discuss how the concept of "Zion" changed over time.

II Samuel 5:7 · Isaiah 2:2–3 · Psalm 149:1-4 · Hebrews 12:22 · Revelation 14:1

Worksheet

1. What is the Scripture reference and date for the Conquest of Jerusalem?

2. Who was Saul's son who some followed as their king?

3. Name the two men who claimed to be king after Saul died. Which regions supported each man?

4. How did David become the one king of Israel?

5. Who was living at the stronghold that David wanted?

6. How did David get into the stronghold to take over?

7. What was the name of the mountain where David took the stronghold?

8. Name three things given to David by the king of Tyre.

9. Why was God blessing David and establishing him as king?

Project 1—Bible Reading

Read about David's conquest of Jerusalem in II Samuel 5. Choosing from the words in the text, fill in the blanks below with the appropriate parts of speech.

Nouns

_____

_____

_____

_____

Verbs

_____

_____

_____

_____

Adjectives

_____

_____

_____

_____

Project 2

In the blank write "R" for righteous if the statement was something with which God was pleased. Write "S" sinful if the statement explains something that is sinful.

_____ The Israelites carried the Ark on poles.
_____ Uzzah touched the Ark to steady it.
_____ David wanted to bring the Ark to Jerusalem.
_____ They sacrificed oxen and sheep every six paces.
_____ The Israelites copied off the pagan Philistines.
_____ David danced before the Lord.
_____ David said he would humble himself even more.
_____ The Israelites transported the Ark on a cart.
_____ The Levites carried the Ark.

The Ark Enthroned in Jerusalem

Worksheet

1. What is the Scripture reference and date for the Ark Enthroned in Jerusalem?

2. How were the Israelites supposed to move the Ark?

3. How did the Israelites wrongly try to move the Ark? From whom were they copying this method?

4. What did Uzzah do? What happened to him?

5. How did God treat the house of Obed-Edom?

6. Describe the sacrifices that David made the second time they moved the Ark.

7. What was David doing as the Ark was brought into Jerusalem?

8. Who did not like David's actions? What was her punishment?

Project 1—Bible Reading

Read in II Samuel 6 about the Ark being brought to Jerusalem. Then complete the word find below and be sure to know what each word has to do with the story.

```
C A R R T S O B E D E D O M A B
I O X A N A S X B H J K L P O I
N I N S T R U M E N T S R T Y U
S Q W T E N S T E N N T S I I X
T S T U M B L D M I C H A E L S
R U D M B U X O M S R D A V I D
U N E B A Z N N E D A S T E N T
M D S L R Z S D M S I X E M I L
N I P E R A M E I S S V E R I S
T G I D R H M S C G I P R E S S
S N S Q E N A P H S N S S S B C
U I C W N B S I A Q S I S S A A
Z F A E Z V D S L W E R F S R R
Z E R R Z C F E B U S T A I R E
I I T T Y X G D A N C E D S E Y
H D O B E D E D O O M N B V N D
```

cart	Obededom	tent
instruments	six	raisins
stumbled	danced	undignified
Uzzah	Michal	barren
oxen	despised	

David Writes Many Psalms

Project 2–Bible Reading

Read Psalm 37. This psalm of David discusses the Heritage of the Righteous and the Calamity of the Wicked, or what will happen to both the righteous and the wicked. In the chart below, write phrases or sentences from the psalm that describe what each will receive.

The Heritage of the Righteous	The Calamity of the Wicked

Worksheet

1. Who wrote many of the Psalms?

2. Name the five types of psalms.

3. Describe psalms of lament.

4. What is an example of a psalm of confession?

5. Describe imprecatory psalms.

6. What is the approximate date of the psalms?

Project 1—Bible Reading

Read Psalms 129, 88, 33, 38, and 9:1-6. Write in the blanks which type of psalm each is. Then answer each question according to the Psalm.

PRAISE _____

What about God is worthy of praise?

THANKSGIVING _____

What has God done for the author?

LAMENT _____

How is the author asking God to help him?

IMPRECATORY _____

Like what does the author ask God to make his enemies?

CONFESSION _____

Name three ways in which sin was affecting the author.

David and Bathsheba

Project 2—Symbolism in Church Art

The picture on the front depicts David seeing Bathsheba take a bath. Yet that is not all that is in the picture. To decode or "read" this illustration it is helpful to know that long ago, when people were creating art for the church, they used colors and animals and shapes to tell stories in pictures for those who could not read. Everyone knew what the symbols represented, just like in our time, everyone knows when they see a golden "M" that it means hamburgers.

Find the following elements in the picture then color in the illustration or create your own picture using some of the ancient church art symbols below.

Dove: A dove is a representation of the Holy Spirit.

Fox: Often symbolizing the Devil, the fox represents cunning and guile. Sin is crouching on David's side of the picture.

Lamb: The lamb is often a symbol for Jesus, but in this picture it is linked with the story Nathan told to David and is the intended prey of the fox.

Nudity: A nude body often was a symbol for purity and innocence.

Three: The number three represents God as he exists in the Trinity (Father, Son and Holy Spirit). What do you see three of in the picture? Hint: In the book of Romans, it is said that we can see things about God even in nature.

Water: Water is usually a symbol of purifying and cleansing due to it's use in Baptism. Sometimes it can symbolize trouble as in Psalm 69:1–2. Here it is being used in this latter way.

Worksheet

1. What is the Scripture reference and date for David and Bathsheba?

2. What was the sin of David and Bathsheba?

3. Who was Bathsheba's husband?

4. How did David first try to hide his sin? Why did that attempt not work?

5. What did David have Joab do?

6. Who then married Bathsheba?

7. Who was Nathan?

8. What happened to the child born from the sinful union of David and Bathsheba?

9. Who was another son born to David and Bathsheba?

Project 1—Bible Reading

Read about the story of David and Bathsheba in II Samuel 11–12. Then answer the following questions.

1. What should David have been doing instead of staying home in Jerusalem?

   _____

2. Why did Uriah sleep at the door of the king's house when he was called home from the war?

   _____

3. David tried a second night to get Uriah to go home. What did David do to Uriah so that he might go home?

   _____

4. Joab put Uriah on the _____ and he was _____.

5. Describe the parable that Nathan told David to show him his sin.

   _____

   _____

Project 2

David wrote Psalm 3 when his son Absalom crowned him-self king. David had lost the loyalty of most of the kingdom and had to flee from Jerusalem. Read Psalm 3. Then draw a picture below of how Absalom was killed.

David and Absalom

Worksheet

1. What is the Scripture reference and date for David and Absalom?

2. Describe Absalom. How was he related to David?

3. How did Absalom steal the hearts of the men of Israel?

4. When Absalom had himself crowned king, what did David do?

5. Who was the follower of David who was sent to give Absalom bad advice?

6. What should Absalom have done when he had David on the run?

7. What did Absalom do?

8. How did Absalom become stuck in the tree?

9. How did Absalom die? Who killed him?

10. How did David react to the death of Absalom?

Project 1—Bible Reading

Read about David and Absalom in II Samuel 15, 18. Then draw three scenes as described by the captions below them. Use conversation bubbles to include the important words that were said.

Absalom steals the hearts of the people
David flees Jerusalem
Absalom's death

Solomon's Reign

Project 2

Read in I Kings 1 about Solomon's brother's attempt to take the throne instead of Solomon. Then write a paragraph about what happened.

_____

_____

_____

_____

_____

_____

_____

Worksheet

1. What is the Scripture reference and date for Solomon's Reign?

2. Who was Solomon's father?

3. What did Solomon request of God?

4. During Solomon's reign there was _____ in Israel.

5. Describe the temple.

6. Who came to visit Solomon to see the temple and his wealth?

7. Late in life Solomon was tempted by _____ and he turned from _____ .

8. How long did Solomon reign?

Project 1—Bible Reading

Many of the proverbs teach lessons about the character of a godly person and a foolish person. Fill the blanks with a word or phrase that describes the character of a godly person.

Prov. 25:16 _____

Prov. 25:17 _____

Prov. 27:18 _____

Prov. 28:27 _____

Prov. 29:11 _____

Prov. 29:20 _____

Prov. 29:23 _____

Many of the proverbs are addressed to a son. While most all of the advice to the son can be applied to women, Proverbs 31 gives a separate description of a woman of excellence. Write the characteristics described in the following verses found in Proverbs 31.

v. 15 _____

v. 16 _____

v. 20 _____

v. 21 _____

v. 25 _____

v. 26 _____

v. 31 _____

Project 2

Read Proverbs 3:1–12. In the verses listed in the left column, look for a word that fits the box outline next to it.

Verse—

3:1

3:2

3:4

3:6

3:10

3:11

Now write below the letters that you placed in the underlined boxes. What word do these letters spell?

_ _ _ _ _

Solomon Given Wisdom

Worksheet

1. What is the Scripture reference and date for Solomon Given Wisdom?

2. What characteristic did Solomon display when God appeared to him?

3. When did God appear to Solomon? What did God ask Solomon?

4. What did Solomon request? Why?

5. What two things did God also give to Solomon along with his request?

6. Why did nobles from far away lands come to visit Solomon?

Project 1—Bible Reading

Read in 1 Kings 3 about Solomon's request for wisdom. Then fill in the spaces below with the details of the case that was brought before Solomon.

The parties involved:

_____

The problem:

_____
_____

Solomon's solution:

_____
_____

How the parties reacted to Solomon's solution:

_____
_____

Solomon's final verdict:

_____
_____

Project 2—Bible Reading

Many of the proverbs use a picture or comparison to teach a lesson. Choose from the four proverbs to illustrate in the boxes below. Write words to label what is being compared to in the picture and circle the reference for the proverb you illustrate.

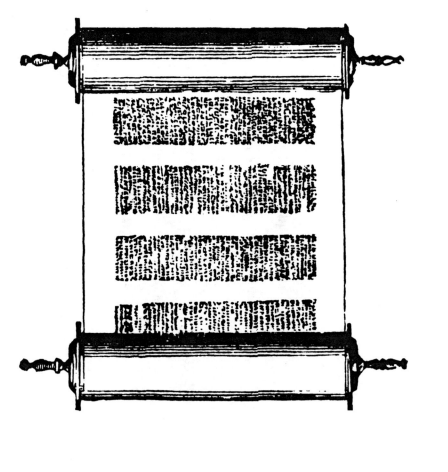

The Writings of Solomon

Worksheet

1. What is the Scripture reference and date for the Writings of Solomon?

2. Name two words that describe what things were like during Solomon's reign.

3. Even more than his father, _____, Solomon was a patron of the _____.

4. About how many proverbs did Solomon write?

5. What is one of the oldest philosophy books in the world?

6. According to Ecclesiastes, what is meaningless?

7. What is man's greatest goal in life according to Ecclesiastes?

Project 1—Bible Reading

A main focus of the Proverbs is to contrast the righteous (wise person) and the wicked (fool). Read Proverbs 10. For each verse on the chart write how the righteous and the wicked are described.

	Righteous	**Wicked**
v. 1		
v. 4		
v. 5		
v. 16		
v. 20		
v. 23		
v. 25		
v. 27		

Project 2—Art for Worship

When God was designing a building for worshipping Him, a very important element was the building's appearance. The book *Art and the Bible* discusses the importance of the visual arts in God's design for the temple: ". . . the temple was filled with artwork. 'And he [Solomon] garnished [covered] the house with precious stones for beauty' (2 Chron. 3:6). Notice this carefully: The temple was covered with precious stones for beauty. There was no pragmatic reason for the precious stones. They had no utilitarian purpose. God simply wanted beauty in the temple. God is interested in beauty." *Read I Kings 6:29 and in the blank write what elements were incorporated into the building of the temple not out of architectural necessity but for the sake of being beautiful. Then design a repeating pattern (like wallpaper) based on your answer in the box at the bottom of the page.*

I Kings 6:29

The Temple is Built

Worksheet

POMEGRANATES.

1. What is the Scripture reference and date for the Temple is Built?

2. From what country did Solomon obtain cedar trees?

3. Name two things that Hiram, king of Tyre provided for Solomon.

4. What did the metal worker do?

5. Describe where the blocks for the temple were cut and fitted.

6. Describe the interior of the temple.

7. The temple was built to be _____ and _____.

8. List three temple decorations.

9. How long did it take for the temple to be built?

10. What happened when God made his presence known inside the new temple?

Project 1—Bible Reading

As you read in 1 Kings 6–8 about the building of the temple, make a list of building supplies (woods and metals) and decorations used in this magnificent architectural structure.

Building Supplies   Decorations

The Queen of Sheba Visits Solomon

Use the code to translate each characteristic of the Queen of Sheba. Then write an explanation of how she displayed that characteristic in the verse listed.

1=A	2=B	3=C	4=D	5=E	6=F	7=G
8=H	9=I	10=J	11=K	12=L	13=M	14=N
15=O	16=P	17=Q	18=R	19=S	20=T	21=U
22=V	23=W	24=X	25=Y	26=Z		

1. 16 15 23 5 18 6 21 12 _____ I Kings 10:1

2. 19 11 5 16 20 9 3 1 12 _____ I Kings 10:1

3. 9 13 16 18 5 19 19 5 4 _____ I Kings 10:4, 5

4. 7 15 4 - 6 5 1 18 9 14 7 _____ I Kings 10:9

5. 7 14 5 18 15 21 19 _____ I Kings 10:10

Worksheet

1. What is the Scripture reference and date for the Queen of Sheba Visits Solomon?

2. Why did the Queen of Sheba visit Solomon?

3. Describe the Queen of Sheba's traveling companions.

4. How did the queen's time with Solomon go?

5. Who did the Queen of Sheba say was blessed because of Solomon's wisdom?

6. What did the Queen of Sheba give to Solomon?

Project 1—Bible Reading

Read in I Kings 10:1-13 about the Queen of Sheba's visit with Solomon. Then fill in the text and crossword puzzle below.

The Queen of (1 across) had heard of Solomon's (2 across). She came to (3 down) his wisdom. She brought many (4 across) loaded with (5 down), gold, and precious stones. The queen (6 across) Solomon about many things. She found that his (7 down) and (8 across) exceeded what she had heard. Both the queen and Solomon gave each other many (9 down) .

Project 2

The End of Solomon's Reign

Fill in the bubbles regions to describe Solomon's reign.

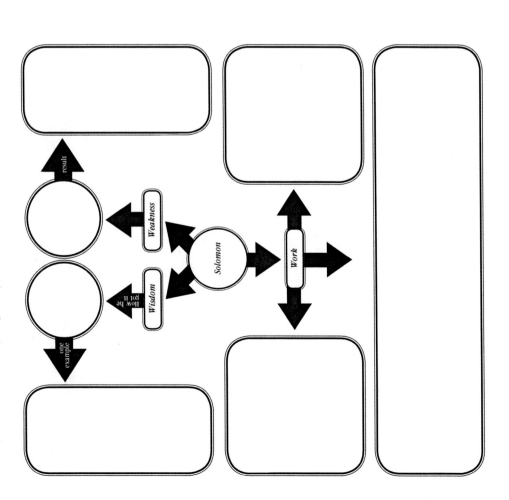

result

Weakness

Wisdom

How he got it

Solomon

Work

one example

Worksheet

1. What is the Scripture reference and date for the end of Solomon's reign?

2. What did Solomon do late in life?

3. Why did God command the Israelites not to make covenants with foreigners?

4. What did Solomon build for his wives?

5. Whom did God raise up against Solomon?

6. What was the greatest punishment Solomon received for his sin?

Project 1—Bible Reading

Read in I Kings 11:1-13 about the end of Solomon's reign. The silly phrases below rhyme with phrases from the story. Write the phrase from the story next to each silly phrase. Then write a sentence using each phrase as it is used in the story. The longer phrases contain small words which are not rhymed. These small words are underlined so that you will know they are not to be changed.

Lauren hives

_____

bye faces

_____

turned intense

_____

learned <u>his</u> part

_____

bear <u>the</u> wisdom today

_____

<u>not</u> delay the cord

_____

Project 2

Israel Divides Into Two Kingdoms

Read I Kings 12:25–33 and then discuss the changes (and the reasons for the changes) made by Jeroboam using the questions below. Color the Northern and Southern Kingdoms different colors:

1. How did Jeroboam establish new places of worship for the North?

2. Why did Jeroboam do this?

3. Why do you think Jeroboam chose the location of those two cities for new worship sites?

4. What three other new things did Jeroboam create or establish?

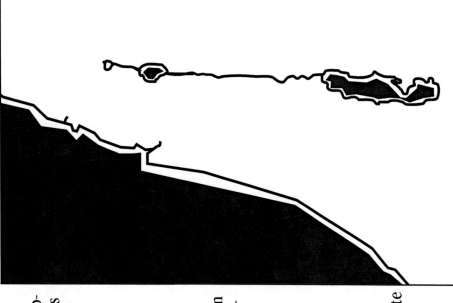

Worksheet

1. What is the Scripture reference and date for Israel Divides into Two Kingdoms?

2. What did Solomon do that angered God?

3. What was the consequence of Solomon's sin?

4. Why wouldn't the punishment come during Solomon's life?

5. Who was Ahijah? What did he do?

6. Why did the tribes rebel against Rehoboam?

7. Who ruled over the ten tribes?

Project 1—Bible Reading

Read the account of the division of Israel in I Kings. Especially take note of how Rehoboam handled his first challenge of being king: the people's request for him to lighten the burden of their work. Then fill in the quotes using your own words to summarize the conversation between Rehoboam, the people, and his advisors.

THE PEOPLE SAID,

"_____"

REHOBOAM SAID,

"_____"

THE OLDER ADVISORS SAID,

"_____"

REHOBOAM SAID,

"_____"

THE YOUNGER ADVISORS SAID,

"_____"

REHOBOAM TOLD THE PEOPLE,

"_____"

THE PEOPLE TOLD REHOBOAM,

"_____"

Project 2

Complete the chart listing the reigns of the kings of Israel. Inside each box is the Scripture reference in which you will find the lengths of their reigns and whether they were good or bad kings. If the king was good put a + (plus) in the box. If the king was bad, put a - (minus) in the box. Write the number of years of the reign in the Length of Reign box.

Kings of Israel

King	Length of Reign		Good or Bad (+ or -)	
Jeroboam	I Kings 14:20		I Kings 14:7,8	
Nadab	I Kings 15:25		I Kings 15:26	
Baasha	I Kings 15:33		I Kings 15:34	
Elah	I Kings 16:8		I Kings 16:13	
Zimri	I Kings 16:15		I Kings 16:19	
Omri	I Kings 16:23		I Kings 16:25	
Ahab	I Kings 16:29		I Kings 16:30	
Ahaziah	I Kings 22:51		I Kings 22:52	
Joram	II Kings 3:1		II Kings 3:2	
Jehu	II Kings 10:36			
Jehoahaz	II Kings 13:1		II Kings 13:2	
Jehoash	II Kings 13:10		II Kings 13:11	
Jeroboam II	II Kings 14:23		II Kings 14:24	
Zechariah	II Kings 15:8		II Kings 15:9	
Shallum	II Kings 15:13			
Menahem	II Kings 15:17		II Kings 15:18	
Pekahiah	II Kings 15:23		II Kings 15:24	
Pekah	II Kings 15:27		II Kings 15:28	
Hoshea	II Kings 17:1		II Kings 17:2	

Worksheet

1. What is the Scripture reference and date for the Kings of Israel?

2. How many tribes did the kings of Israel rule?

3. In what region of the old unified Israel did the kings of the divided Israel rule?

4. How was Israel less faithful than Judah? What was the consequence of Israel's unfaithfulness in this area?

5. Who was the first king of Israel after the division?

6. How righteous were the kings of Israel?

7. What is tribute?

8. What nation conquered Israel?

9. Name one evidence that the nation was weak close to the time when it fell.

Project 1—Bible Reading

In I Kings 15:33–16:34 you will read about the reigns of four kings of Israel. All of these kings are wicked. Watch for a phrase that God uses over and over to describe them as evil. (Hint: He compares the wicked king to another wicked king.) Write the name of the king of Israel that fits each description.

1. Burned the king's house down upon himself
   _____

2. Was drunk when he was killed
   _____

3. Moved the capital to Samaria
   _____

4. Killed all of the house of Baasha
   _____

5. Was told that dogs or birds would eat his family when they died
   _____

6. Built the city of Samaria
   _____

7. Was visited by Jehu the prophet
   _____

8. Half of the people followed Tibni instead of him
   _____

9. What phrase commonly describes wicked kings?
   (1 Kings 15:34, 16:19, 16:26)
   _____

Project 2

Complete the chart listing the reigns of the kings of Judah. Inside each box is a Scripture reference in which you will find the length of their reign and whether they were good or bad kings. If the king was good, put a + (plus) in the box. If the king was bad, put a - (minus) in the box. Write the length of the reign in the box.

Kings of Judah

King	Length of Reign		Good or Bad (+ or -)	
Rehoboam	I Kings 14:21		I Kings 14:22	
Abijam	I Kings 15:2		I Kings 15:3	
Asa	I Kings 15:9		I Kings 15:11	
Jehoshaphat	I Kings 22:42		I Kings 22:43	
Jehoram	II Kings 8:17		II Kings 8:18,19	
Ahaziah	II Kings 8:26		II Kings 8:27	
Athaliah	II Kings 11:3		II Kings 11:1	
Joash	II Kings 12:1		II Kings 12:2	
Amaziah	II Kings 14:2		II Kings 14:3	
Azariah	II Kings 15:2		II Kings 15:3	
Jotham	II Kings 15:33		II Kings 15:34	
Ahaz	II Kings 16:2		II Kings 16:2	
Hezekiah	II Kings 18:2		II Kings 18:3	
Manasseh	II Kings 21:1		II Kings 21:2	
Amon	II Kings 21:19		II Kings 21:20	
Josiah	II Kings 21:1		II Kings 21:2	
Jehoahaz	II Kings 23:31		II Kings 23:32	
Jehoiakim	II Kings 23:36		II Kings 23:37	
Jehoiachin	II Kings 24:8		II Kings 24:9	
Zedekiah	II Kings 24:18		II Kings 24:19	

Worksheet

1. What is the Scripture reference and date for the Kings of Judah?

2. Who was the first king of Judah after it split with Israel?

3. Why did the people rebel against their first king?

4. To whom was the first king related?

5. Which two tribes were ruled by the kings of Judah?

6. What happened during Asa's reign? Why?

7. Why did God put off his judgment on Judah for a time?

8. God was gracious on Judah to grant _____ reigns to the righteous kings.

9. What nation conquered Judah?

Project 1—Bible Reading

Read about the lives of two of the kings of Judah. Then under the heading of Good and Bad list some of the good and bad things that each king did.

ASA: II CHRONICLES 14–16

GOOD

1. _____
2. _____
3. _____

BAD

1. _____
2. _____
3. _____

AZARIAH (ALSO CALLED UZZIAH): II CHRONICLES 26

GOOD

1. _____
2. _____
3. _____

BAD

1. _____
2. _____
3. _____